ESSAYS IN INTERNATIONAL FINANCE

No. 186, April 1992

GROWTH AND CATCH-UP IN CENTRAL AND EASTERN EUROPE: MACROECONOMIC EFFECTS ON WESTERN COUNTRIES

ALESSANDRO GIUSTINIANI

FRANCESCO PAPADIA

AND

DANIELA PORCIANI

INTERNATIONAL FINANCE SECTION

DEPARTMENT OF ECONOMICS
PRINCETON UNIVERSITY
PRINCETON, NEW JERSEY

ESSAYS IN INTERNATIONAL FINANCE

ESSAYS IN INTERNATIONAL FINANCE are published by the International Finance Section of the Department of Economics of Princeton University. The Section sponsors this series of publications, but the opinions expressed are those of the authors. The Section welcomes the submission of manuscripts for publication in this and its other series. Please see the Notice to Contributors at the back of this Essay.

Francesco Papadia, Alessandro Giustiniani, and Daniela Porciani all worked in the Research Department of the Banca d'Italia while writing this Essay. Francesco Papadia, then Head of the Bank's International Economy Sector, now manages its Foreign Department. Alessandro Giustiniani, Senior Economist at the Bank, is now Technical Assistant to the Executive Director for Italy at the International Monetary Fund. Daniela Porciani continues as Research Assistant at the Bank.

GIUSEPPE BERTOLA, *Acting Director*
International Finance Section

ESSAYS IN INTERNATIONAL FINANCE

No. 186, April 1992

GROWTH AND CATCH-UP IN CENTRAL AND EASTERN EUROPE: MACROECONOMIC EFFECTS ON WESTERN COUNTRIES

ALESSANDRO GIUSTINIANI

FRANCESCO PAPADIA

AND

DANIELA PORCIANI

INTERNATIONAL FINANCE SECTION

DEPARTMENT OF ECONOMICS
PRINCETON UNIVERSITY
PRINCETON, NEW JERSEY

Library of Congress Cataloging-in-Publication Data

Giustiniani, Alessandro
Growth and catch-up in Central and Eastern Europe: macroeconomic effects on western countries / Alessandro Giustiniani, Francesco Papadia, and Daniela Porciani.
p. cm.—(Essays in international finance, ISSN 0071-142X ; no. 186)
Includes bibliographical references.
ISBN 0-88165-093-5 (pbk.) : $6.50
1. Economic assistance—Europe, Eastern. 2. Europe, Eastern—Economic conditions—1989- I. Papadia, Francesco. II. Porciani, Daniela. III. Title. IV. Series.
HG136.P7 no. 186
338.947—dc20
332.1′5—dc20 92-13314
CIP

Printed in the United States of America by Princeton University Press at Princeton, New Jersey

International Standard Serial Number: 0071-142X
International Standard Book Number: 0-88165-093-5
Library of Congress Catalog Card Number: 92-13314

CONTENTS

LIST OF TABLES

LIST OF FIGURES

GROWTH AND CATCH-UP IN CENTRAL AND EASTERN EUROPE: MACROECONOMIC EFFECTS ON WESTERN COUNTRIES

1 Introduction

The last two years have seen a radical transformation of Central and Eastern Europe. The *ancien régime* has collapsed and a democratic society, based on the tenets of the market economy, has begun to take shape.[1] When the exciting news began to arrive from beyond the Iron Curtain, a situation of pure Knightian uncertainty prevailed, with no *a priori* or empirical basis for forecasting future developments. Now, thanks to massive investment from the economics industry, we have reached a state that (drawing from Knight) we may define as risk. Indeed, the potential scenarios are becoming more definite, as are the circumstances that will determine whether one scenario or another will prevail.[2]

The various scenarios result from combining the answers to five basic questions. First and foremost is the question of structural reforms—whether Eastern European countries will manage to carry out, in an environment of relative macroeconomic stability, the far-reaching

This paper is dedicated to the memory of Stefano Vona whose comments, criticism, and help we missed so much. The authors are grateful to P. Catte, C. De Vincenti, M. Draghi, W. Gebauer, A. Gelb, T. Krueger, M. Marrese, J. Mélitz, G. Meredith, G. Szegö, U. Thumm, C. Wyplosz, and an anonymous referee for their helpful comments, and to G. Meredith, M. McGregor, and J.C. Martinez Oliva for help in handling the INTERMOD world model. The authors are naturally responsible for any remaining mistakes and shortcomings, and the views expressed are not necessarily those of any of the above or of the Banca d'Italia. The programs and data used in this paper are available from the authors on request.

[1] The terms "Central" and "Eastern European" economies are used in this essay to indicate the economies of Czechoslovakia, Hungary, Poland, Romania, Bulgaria, the former Soviet Union, and the former German Democratic Republic (GDR), now part of unified Germany.

[2] See Fitoussi and Phelps (1990) and Wyplosz (1991) for a theoretical framework clarifying the various possible outcomes.

reforms needed to transform their economies (see G-10, 1991, on this issue). Second, third, and fourth are the questions of labor, capital, and goods mobility. The consequences will be very different depending on whether massive migration from Eastern to Western Europe occurs or is stemmed by its natural costs or by explicit migration policies; whether capital moves freely to Eastern Europe in search of a higher return or is hindered by natural and man-made imperfections; and whether trade is relatively free, so that countries can specialize on the basis of their comparative advantages, or is limited and distorted by protectionism. The fifth and last question is whether Western industrial countries will accommodate, through macroeconomic policies, the additional demand generated by the reconstruction process in the East.

This essay provides a quantitative description of two of the scenarios that might result from specific combinations of the answers to the five questions above. It aims at estimating the potential demand by the Central and Eastern European countries for foreign resources connected with investment to catch up to Western economic standards and the macroeconomic consequences for Western economies of this increased demand. In both of our scenarios, the reform process in the East is taken to be successful and labor to be basically immobile, whereas capital and tradable goods are assumed to move freely between the two areas. The two scenarios differ in that the second assumes that Western economies accommodate the additional demand coming from the East by increasing domestic saving through budget-deficit reductions.

We are aware that our approach is limited by three basic problems. First, the statistical information about the present state of Eastern economies is very uncertain, even for an indicator as fundamental as national income. Second, because the Eastern economies are undergoing far-reaching structural changes, the parameters needed to obtain the required estimates cannot be derived from past information but must be approximated. Third, for lack of a world model explicitly encompassing the economies of Central and Eastern Europe, the exercise is essentially recursive: the import requirements of the East are estimated and allowed to affect Western economies, but there is no feed-back to the East.

This essay is organized in the following manner. By comparing several indicators, Section 2 shows that human capital in Central and Eastern Europe can be considered broadly similar to that of Western Europe, in particular to that of its southern part. In Section 3, the import requirements arising from the reform and reconstruction process are estimated. For this purpose, each Eastern country has been matched with a Western counterpart represented by a single country or by the average of a group of countries chosen on the basis of human-capital indicators and geographical propinquity. These criteria have allowed us to match Western to Eastern countries in such a way that excessively wide productivity gaps have been avoided. It has then been assumed that, in a number of years, each Eastern country will share some basic characteristics with its Western counterpart, particularly with regard to labor productivity.[3] This will be brought about by very rapid "technological progress" and by increasing the capital-to-labor ratio. The investment needed to achieve this increase is translated into import requirements by making some bold assumptions about the behavior of key Eastern national-accounting variables, especially consumption. For each Eastern country, the duration of the catch-up period has been chosen on the basis of the country's position in the process of reform, while avoiding unrealistically high rates of productivity growth.

The resulting import requirements are very large, notwithstanding the fact that many parameters of the exercise have been chosen in order to obtain a lower rather than a higher estimate.[4] The additional combined net-import requirement is equal to about $54 billion in the first year of the simulation and grows to a peak of $312 billion in the ninth year.[5] The net-import requirement returns to zero in the sixteenth year, after which the Eastern countries' trade balances turn into surpluses that grow very large in the final years of our simulation. The additional demand from the East is not only very large in the first years of the simulation but also heavily concentrated on the former West Germany, which would have to export nearly $106 billion more in the peak year (about 33 percent of the total shock). At the other

[3] During the 1960s, a lively debate developed among economists and sociologists on the issue raised by Tinbergen (1961) concerning the convergence of centrally planned and market economies. But nowadays the ongoing process "is not a convergence of both capitalism and socialism toward some median optimal order but a one-sided convergence of centrally planned economies toward western-style market economies." (Roland, 1990, p. 385) On the convergence theory, see, for example, Lauterbach (1976), Spulber and Horowitz (1976), and Ellman (1984).

[4] In a previous version of this paper (1991), we followed a similar approach, though with different hypotheses and estimation procedures. The estimated import requirements were much higher. That paper can be used as a sort of rough sensitivity analysis of the exercise presented here, showing what would happen if the import requirements were higher.

[5] Unless otherwise indicated, dollar amounts are at 1989 prices.

extreme, the United States would experience an additional demand of less than $6 billion in the peak year (about 2 percent of the total).

In Section 4, the estimated import requirements are applied to the Western economies using the INTERMOD model.[6] As might be expected, the results show quite significant macroeconomic strains: large increases in interest rates and inflation, significant exchange-rate fluctuations, and crowding out of domestic demand and production. It is shown in Section 5, however, that the macroeconomic strains are significantly diminished if governments cut their expenditures so as to offset half the additional demand shock. In any event, the increase in productivity of the Eastern countries benefits Western economies as well by producing large investment-income inflows.

The actual import requirements may well be larger than those estimated in this essay; in addition, the cuts in government expenditure necessary to avoid macroeconomic strains will be substantial in some Western countries (especially Germany) and may be difficult to implement. What will also be required, as an additional line of defence, is that Western countries pursue determined policies of trade liberalization to increase the substitutability of the goods they produce and thus to spread the demand shock more evenly across the industrial countries.

Our estimates should not be interpreted as absolute or central-tendency forecasts, but rather as forecasts conditional on the basic assumptions noted above: thorough reform in the East, no labor mobility, and perfect goods and capital mobility between the West and the East.[7] Some of these conditioning factors are meta-economic, having a strong policy component. Prominent among them is the political ability to carry out the complex and difficult actions needed to reform the Eastern economies, to open Western markets to Eastern goods, and to keep wage costs in the East in line with productivity (which implies

[6] INTERMOD is described by Meredith (1989) and Masson and Meredith (1990). It is a PC version of MULTIMOD, the world model built at the International Monetary Fund (see Masson, Symansky, and Meredith, 1990), and is a small model of the economies of the Group of Eight (G-8) countries especially designed for simulation purposes. Special care was taken to achieve acceptable long-run characteristics and to take account of both stocks and flows.

[7] The hypothesis of perfect capital mobility is clearly wrong, as is any simplifying hypothesis used to move from the bewildering complexity and variety of the real world to manageable analyses useful for orienting policy. The questions are whether the hypothesis is *so* wrong as to void the analysis of any value and whether there is a dominant hypothesis to substitute for it.

measures to avoid large-scale labor migration). The assumption of perfect capital mobility likewise implies policy actions that foster it, such as the catalyzing activities of international financial institutions, but it also implies a view about the working of the world economy. The relative and unexpected ease with which world capital markets adjusted in the 1980s to the huge and sustained current-account deficits of the United States and the corresponding surpluses of Japan and West Germany proves that capital is much more mobile than any observer predicted at the beginning of the last decade, reminding one of the mobility observed at the turn of the last century with regard to financing the large and sustained deficits of Canada. This does not imply, however, that one can dismiss the arguments, raised most forcefully by Collins and Rodrik (1991), about the elements that could limit the flow of capital toward the East.[8]

More generally, in judging the plausibility of the scenarios presented in this essay, the reader should bear in mind that any scenario resulting from such an extreme event as the recent revolution in Eastern Europe risks looking unrealistic. A scenario of continuing poverty in Eastern Europe, contrasting with affluence in Western Europe and generating massive pressure to migrate, is not, in our view, more plausible than the one of catch-up presented here. What this essay hopes to contribute is a thoroughly worked out estimate of two possible scenarios that are both desirable from a welfare point of view and which adequate policy actions in East and West can promote.

2 Human Capital in the East

It is widely recognized that the potential quality of labor inputs in Central and Eastern Europe is reasonably high (see OECD, 1990b, and CEPR, 1990); however, the distorted economic system has depressed the return on human capital, one of the fundamental driving forces of economic development. This is vividly illustrated by Figures 1 and 2. Figure 1 shows the data on life expectancy at birth and (the log of) per capita income reported by the United Nations Development Programme (1990) for about 130 countries. As shown by the interpolated line,

[8] Collins and Rodrik also criticize the needs-based approach for its assumption that all investment for catch-up will have to be financed from abroad. We do not follow this course of analysis in this essay but instead derive our external deficits from a complete, though extremely simplified, national-accounting framework. We also assume very high savings rates in the Eastern countries, which help finance the massive investment.

FIGURE 1

LIFE EXPECTANCY AND PER CAPITA GROSS DOMESTIC PRODUCT
(in years and U.S. dollars)

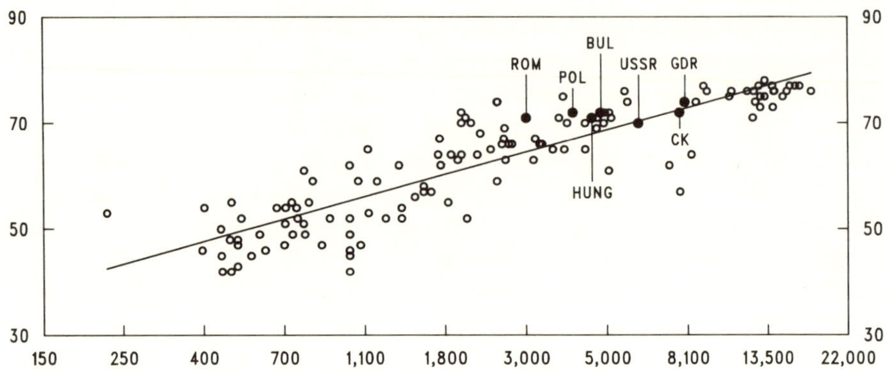

FIGURE 2

ADULT LITERACY AND PER CAPITA GROSS DOMESTIC PRODUCT
(in percentage points and U.S. dollars)

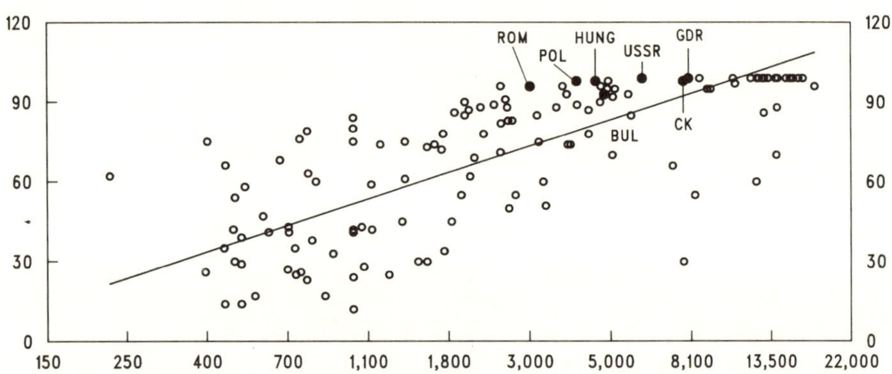

there is a strong positive relation between the two variables. However, the Central and Eastern European countries are characterized by a level of per capita income lower than warranted by their high life expectancy. An analogous conclusion can be drawn from Figure 2, which shows the relation, admittedly noisier, between the literacy rate and (the log of) per capita income.

Human capital is a very complex variable that cannot be measured precisely by simple indicators like those used above.[9] We have therefore tried to give more content to our analysis by considering eight other human-capital proxies relating to education and health. In Table 1, the Eastern European countries are compared with 16 reference countries: 12 Western European and 4 developing. A black cell for a variable indicates that the Eastern country has a better or equal value than the reference country; an asterisk indicates a missing value. Reference countries are ordered from top to bottom according to the number of white cells, that is, according to their relative human-capital endowments. Looking at the distribution of black and white cells, we can tentatively deduce that the human-capital endowments of the Central and Eastern European countries are broadly comparable to those of middle-ranking Western European countries.

Notwithstanding this similarity, it is obvious that the implementation of even the most successful reforms will not allow an instantaneous jump in the return to human capital and that considerable time will be needed for a learning-by-doing process. There is a basic relation between human capital and growth, however, and the works of Romer (1989b) and Lucas (1988) are breathing new life into it. Indeed, these and other authors are developing fascinating new perspectives on economic growth based on the idea that, once external effects are considered, accumulation gives rise to increasing rather than decreasing returns to scale.[10]

Our paper does not follow this line of thought but is not inconsistent with it. Indeed, in our framework, technological progress (albeit formally exogenous) goes together with intense capital accumulation, so that the capital-to-output ratio does not change drastically. This is a historical regularity (see, for example, Maddison, 1987, and Romer, 1989b), which we maintain in our work, although we do not attempt to provide an explanation for it.

3 Economic Growth and Convergence: A Scenario

Studies of long-run productivity trends in industrialized countries have revealed the presence of a convergence phenomenon in both labor

[9] See Becker (1975), Maddison (1979), and Denison (1967) for an analysis of the many facets of human capital and its relation to economic growth.

[10] On the issue of increasing returns to scale, see also Romer (1986, 1987, 1989a) and Baldwin (1989a, 1989b).

TABLE 1
Main Human-Capital Indicators

Bulgaria	1	2	3	4	5	6	7	8
Denmark								
Finland								
Sweden							*	
Italy								*
France								
Austria								
Netherlands								
FRG								
Greece								
Portugal								*
Spain								
Turkey								*
Mexico								
Brazil							*	
India					*			
Nigeria								*

Czechoslovakia	1	2	3	4	5	6	7	8
Denmark								
Finland								
Sweden							*	
Italy								*
France								
Austria								
Netherlands								
FRG								
Greece								
Portugal								*
Spain								
Turkey								
Mexico								
Brazil							*	
India					*			
Nigeria								*

GDR	1	2	3	4	5	6	7	8
Denmark								*
Finland								*
Sweden							*	*
Italy								*
France								*
Austria								*
Netherlands								*
FRG								*
Greece								*
Portugal								*
Spain								*
Turkey								*
Mexico								*
Brazil							*	*
India					*			*
Nigeria								*

Hungary	1	2	3	4	5	6	7	8
Denmark								
Finland								
Sweden							*	
Italy								*
France								
Austria								
Netherlands								
FRG								
Greece								
Portugal								*
Spain								
Turkey								
Mexico								
Brazil							*	
India					*			
Nigeria								*

Poland	1	2	3	4	5	6	7	8
Denmark								
Finland								
Sweden							*	
Italy								*
France								
Austria								
Netherlands								
FRG								
Greece								
Portugal								*
Spain								
Turkey								
Mexico								
Brazil							*	
India					*			
Nigeria								*

Romania	1	2	3	4	5	6	7	8
Denmark						*		*
Finland						*		*
Sweden						*	*	*
Italy						*		*
France						*		*
Austria						*		*
Netherlands						*		*
FRG						*		*
Greece						*		*
Portugal						*		*
Spain						*		*
Turkey						*		*
Mexico						*		*
Brazil						*	*	*
India					*	*		*
Nigeria						*		*

USSR	1	2	3	4	5	6	7	8
Denmark					*		*	
Finland					*		*	
Sweden					*		*	
Italy					*		*	*
France					*		*	
Austria					*		*	
Netherlands					*		*	
FRG					*		*	
Greece					*		*	
Portugal					*		*	*
Spain					*		*	
Turkey					*		*	
Mexico					*		*	
Brazil					*		*	
India					*		*	
Nigeria					*		*	

(1) Life expectancy at birth
(2) Infant mortality rate
(3) Population per physician
(4) Secondary-school enrollment
(5) Percentage of tertiary-school students in science & engineering
(6) Primary-school students per teacher
(7) Secondary-school students per teacher
(8) Percentage of students reaching fourth grade

NOTE: An asterisk indicates the statistic is not available for the country considered.

SOURCE: World Bank, *World Development Report 1989* (1990).

productivity and per capita income.[11] Baumol (1986, p. 1073) finds that "there is a strong inverse correlation between a country's productivity standing in 1970 and its average rate of productivity growth since then. Postwar data suggest that the convergence phenomenon also extends to both 'intermediate' and centrally planned economies. Only the poorer less developed countries show no such trend."

These results can be interpreted in the standard setting of neoclassical growth theory, using the same production function for all countries. Poorer economies have less capital per worker, and the law of diminishing returns implies that they will have a higher rate of return on capital. If there is no restriction on capital mobility, capital will therefore move from rich to poor economies.[12] This, in turn, implies that poor economies will tend to grow faster than rich ones and catch them up in productivity.

We apply this interpretive setting to the Central and Eastern European economies. In particular, we assume that the ongoing reform process will remove barriers to the efficient allocation of resources, as by reducing the proportion of nonperforming investment.[13] This will cause an increase in the return on capital and, over time, in the capital-to-labor ratio, which will bring labor productivity up toward the levels prevailing in the West. The aim of our exercise is to determine the amount of foreign saving that will be necessary to finance this process.

The Methodology

In the first step of our exercise, each Eastern country has been matched with one or more Western countries, which will be the pole of attraction for the Eastern country. In matching countries, we have taken into account, to the extent possible, human-capital information

[11] See, for example, Abramovitz (1979), Baumol (1986), Chenery (1986), Englander and Mittelstadt (1988), Goldsmith (1985), Maddison (1979, 1982, 1987), Wolff (1987), and Larre and Torres (1991). Barro and Sala i Martin (1990) find that the United States provides clear evidence of convergence in the sense that poor economies tend to grow faster than rich economies in per capita terms.

[12] The capital flow to poor economies also implies the diffusion of technological knowledge from the leading economies, which will generate additional gains in productivity (see, for example, Kuznets, 1973).

[13] These issues are briefly analyzed in the Appendix, using a simple two-period, two-country growth model. This model captures the striking association of high rates of investment with low rates of output growth that has been a feature of the Eastern European countries.

(as shown in Table 1), other broad national characteristics, and geographical location. In some cases, however, we have been forced to choose a counterpart country poorer than the one suggested by these criteria in order to avoid excessive productivity gaps between the Western and Eastern countries.

The outcome of this, partly arbitrary, procedure and the resulting productivity gaps between the countries are reported in Table 2. The figures show that labor productivity is very low in the Eastern countries relative to the reference countries, but the numbers are subject to wide margins of uncertainty because of the poor quality of Eastern economic statistics. Except for the former German Democratic Republic (GDR), we use, in our exercise, International Monetary Fund (IMF) estimates of the Eastern countries' gross domestic product (GDP) converted into U.S. dollars at the prevailing commercial exchange rates. In the absence of any official estimate for East Germany, we have approximated the level of GDP in 1989 by assuming that productivity in the GDR was 35 percent of that in the Federal Republic of Germany ([FRG] see, Lipschitz and McDonald, 1990, p. 3). To avoid such cumbersome expressions as the "Eastern region of Germany" or "the former German Democratic Republic," we have retained the use of the terms GDR and FRG to refer to the two regions of the unified Germany. This use also implies that references to "exports of Germany" includes intra-German trade. More generally, the results are given as if unification had not occurred. This assumption is not at all innocuous, and, in a few instances below, we shall have to qualify our results to reflect this unavoidable limitation.

TABLE 2

PRODUCTIVITY GAPS BETWEEN EASTERN AND WESTERN EUROPEAN COUNTRIES IN 1989

Eastern European Countries	Western Reference Countries	Productivity of East as % of West
Bulgaria	Greece, Portugal, and Spain	27
Czechoslovakia	Austria, Greece, Portugal, and Spain	28
GDR	FRG	35
Hungary	Greece, Portugal, and Spain	26
Poland	Greece, Portugal, and Spain	21
Romania	Greece and Portugal	40
USSR[a]	Greece and Portugal	30

[a] For simplicity, we use "USSR" to refer to the countries of the former Soviet Union.

TABLE 3

ALTERNATIVE ESTIMATES OF GROSS DOMESTIC PRODUCT IN THE EASTERN EUROPEAN COUNTRIES IN 1989

(in billions of U.S. dollars and percentages)

	IMF	WEFA		ALTON		PlanEcon[a]	
	(1)	(2)	% (1/2)	(3)	% (1/3)	(4)	% (1/4)
Bulgaria	21.6	50.9	42.4	50.9	42.4	51.3	42.1
Czechoslovakia	50.1	121.4	41.3	122.8	40.8	123.3	40.6
GDR	130.8	188.0	69.6	159.4	82.1	158.2	82.7
Hungary	28.9	72.9	39.6	64.6	44.7	64.7	44.7
Poland	66.8	215.1	31.1	172.9	38.6	173.9	38.4
Romania	53.5	92.0	58.2	105.5	50.7	79.8	67.2
USSR	516.4	2,034.7	25.4	n.a.	n.a.	1,438.4	35.9

[a] Data refer to Gross National Product.

As shown in Table 3, the data that we use, reported in the first column, are significantly lower than those produced by WEFA (1990), Alton et al. (1990), and PlanEcon (1990); the case of the Soviet Union is particularly striking. Our figures also imply estimates of per capita GDP levels that are substantially lower than those reported by Summers and Heston (1988) for 1985. Experience with the GDR after unification, however, seems to confirm the lower rather than the higher estimates for production potential in the East.

In order to determine the amount of foreign saving needed to finance the catch-up of the Eastern economies vis-à-vis their respective counterparts, we start from a simple neoclassic growth model. We assume, for convenience, that the production function in the Eastern economies can be represented by a standard Cobb-Douglas production function:

$$Q_t = A_t K_{t-1}^{\alpha} L_t^{1-\alpha} , \qquad (1)$$

in which Q is the flow of output, A is the total factor productivity (TFP), K is the stock of capital, L is the labor force, and α is the share of capital in total product, which has been assumed to be equal to 0.3 for all the countries on the basis of information reported in Nuti (1988) and Maddison (1987). Output is thus assumed to grow as the result of the long-term effects of technological change, capital accumulation, and labor-force expansion, that is,

$$D\ln Q = D\ln A + \alpha D\ln K + (1 - \alpha)D\ln L \; , \tag{2}$$

in which D denotes the operator d/dt and ln is the natural logarithm operator.

One crucial assumption in our exercise is that capital is mobile but labor is not. Labor mobility would substantially change the results (see Wyplosz, 1991).

We also assume that the rate of growth of labor productivity ($D\ln q \equiv D\ln Q - D\ln L$) in each Eastern country follows over time a modified Rayleigh function,[14] that is,

$$D\ln q^E = \ln\left(1 + g_q^W\right) + \left(\ln q_0^W - \ln q_0^E\right)\left(\frac{t}{\tau^2}\right)\exp\left(-\frac{t^2}{2\tau^2}\right), \tag{3}$$

in which the superscripts E and W indicate the Eastern and the Western country, respectively, g_q^W is the constant growth rate of labor productivity in the Western country,[15] and τ indicates the time when the growth rate reaches its maximum.[16] It can be demonstrated that $D\ln q^E$ will assume the value $\ln(1 + g_q^W)$ both when t is equal to zero and when t approaches infinity. Integrating equation (3), we obtain the following expression for the log of the labor productivity of the Eastern country:

$$\begin{aligned} \ln q_t^E &= \ln q_0^E + \ln\left(1 + g_q^W\right)t \\ &+ \left[\ln q_0^W - \ln q_0^E\right]\left[1 - \exp\left(-\frac{t^2}{2\tau^2}\right)\right]. \end{aligned} \tag{4}$$

[14] On the properties of the Rayleigh distribution function, see Papoulis (1965).

[15] In the case of the Western country, we extrapolate labor productivity by applying the average rate of growth experienced in the period from 1976 to 1989. If more than one Western country is taken into account, we create a synthetic reference country with an initial level and rate of growth of labor productivity equal to the average of the component countries.

[16] In the exercise, τ has been determined exogenously by taking into account, the position of the country concerned in the reform process, the size of the initial productivity gap, and the need to avoid implausibly high productivity growth rates (which would be reflected in exceptionally high rates of capital accumulation).

Accordingly, as shown in Figure 3, the (log of) the Eastern country's productivity rises at an increasing rate until time τ, when the curve bends toward the reference country's productivity curve. The number of years required for the Eastern economy to catch up to the Western economy will depend on the value given to τ; the lower it is, the higher the (initial) average rate of productivity growth will be and the shorter the catch-up period.

FIGURE 3

SMOOTH CONVERGING PATH OF LABOR PRODUCTIVITY

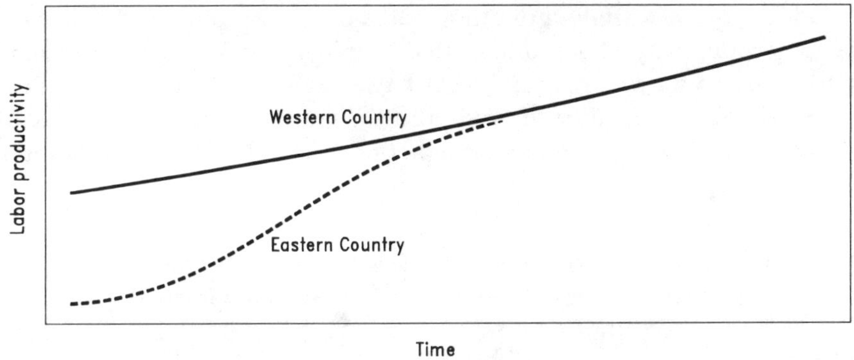

In the framework of neoclassical growth theory, two factors contribute to the growth rate of productivity required for catch-up: capital accumulation and technological progress. To figure out their relative roles, we first determine the initial level of TFP in each Eastern country as a percentage of Italian TFP in 1989.[17] We then assume that the growth rate of each Eastern country's TFP follows the same qualitative path as labor productivity and that it converges toward $(1 - \alpha)D\ln q^E$ in order to stabilize the long-run capital-output ratio in a range between 2 and 3. In choosing the parameters for this exercise, we have also taken into account the experience of countries such as Japan, Germany, Italy, and Greece, all of which experienced in the 1960s a period of very rapid growth in their catch-up toward the technological frontier represented by the United States (Table 4).[18] In particular, we have chosen parameters with a view to avoiding growth rates of labor productivity, TFP,

[17] The TFP of Italy in 1989 is used as a scale factor; it has been estimated by assuming that the Italian production function is Cobb-Douglas with $\alpha = 0.3$.

[18] On this issue, see, for example, Baumol (1986), Goldsmith (1985), Chenery (1986), Wolff (1987), Englander (1988), and Englander and Mittelstadt (1988).

and capital that are out of line with those of the top performers mentioned above. The analogy between these countries after World War II and the Eastern countries resides in the drastic political changes affecting both and in the fact that these changes are associated with reconstruction and the reintegration of their economies into the world economy. The two groups differ substantially, however, with respect to their starting economic structures. In Western Europe, the tenets of a market economy were deeply rooted, even though repressed for several years by autarkic policies and the exigencies of war. In Eastern Europe, the economies seem to have been seriously damaged by forty or more years of central planning.

Once we have specified the time paths of labor productivity and total factor productivity and assumed that employment grows at a constant rate equal to its average for the last twenty years (in practice, nearly zero), we can easily infer the required time path of the capital stock by simply inverting the production function. To obtain gross-investment

TABLE 4

PRODUCTIVITY AND OUTPUT AND INPUT GROWTH IN SOME WESTERN COUNTRIES

(average percentage changes in the business sector at annual rates)

	Output	Total Factor Productivity	Labor Productivity	Capital Productivity	Capital
Japan					
1960-1973	9.7	6.1	8.6	–2.4	12.1
1973-1986	3.8	1.7	3.0	–2.5	6.3
FRG					
1960-1973	4.6	2.8	4.9	–1.1	5.6
1973-1986	2.0	1.3	2.7	–1.2	3.2
Italy					
1960-1973	5.6	4.7	6.5	0.4	5.2
1973-1986	2.4	1.1	1.8	–0.6	2.9
Greece					
1960-1973	8.4	6.6	9.1	–3.4	11.8
1973-1986	2.3	0.6	1.6	–3.3	5.9
OECD[a]					
1960-1973	5.2	2.8	4.1	–0.4	5.6
1973-1986	2.6	0.6	1.5	–1.4	4.0

SOURCE: Englander and Mittelstadt (1988).

[a] Average of member countries.

flows, then, we impose a declining rate of capital depreciation.[19] This reflects the legitimate hypothesis that the Eastern economies will have to scrap a significant part of their obsolete capital stock in the first years of the catch-up process.

The methodology described so far allows us to circumvent the problem that available estimates of existing capital stocks are unreliable; obsolete technologies and wrong relative prices cause overestimates of the stock of economically productive capital in the East. A great deal of anecdotal information is available on the poor state of the capital stock in Eastern Europe and the former Soviet Union. This information is broadly consistent with the findings of Bergson (1987) that labor productivity in the USSR, Hungary, Poland, and Yugoslavia is between one-third and one-quarter lower than in the West, controlling for different levels of capital and land per worker.[20] This evidence can be interpreted to mean that part of the physical capital recorded as available in the East is not economically productive and thus contributes to low labor productivity.

Given national production and investment, we have next to estimate consumption in order to derive net-import requirements from the basic national-accounting identity. For simplicity, and for lack of reliable data, we do not distinguish between private and public consumption. This allows us implicitly to take account of the possible shift between them, because any reduction in public consumption, as the result of lower military expenses, for instance, may be offset by an increase in private consumption to satisfy pent-up consumer demand. Furthermore, we assume that aggregate consumption is kept constant, as a fraction of gross *national* product (GNP), at its estimated level in 1989. This implies a fairly high saving rate, ranging in 1989 from between 22 percent in the former GDR and nearly 34 percent in Romania—with an overall average of 30 percent—against an average of 22 percent in

[19] In the estimation exercise, we assume that the rate of depreciation declines linearly from 7 to 4 percent between the beginning and the fifteenth year of the catch-up period and remains constant thereafter.

[20] By contrast, Burkett and Skegro (1989, p. 1130) estimate constant elasticity of substitution (CES) and translog functions for national income from data on sixty-five countries in 1975 and conclude that "while the relative productivity of socialist economies may decline as capital-labor ratios rise, the net effect of socialism on productivity is insignificantly different from zero at all observed levels of the capital-labor ratio."

the OECD countries. National saving thus contributes significantly to finance the catch-up process. GNP is obtained by deducting factor-service payments from GDP. Because we cannot distinguish between borrowing and direct investment as sources of financing for current-account deficits, we have assumed that factor-service payments at time *t* are given by the stock of external liabilities (both debt and foreign-owned capital) at time $t - 1$ multiplied by a (constant) rate of return. The latter is set equal to the steady-state level of the U.S. long-run real interest rate in the baseline of INTERMOD (4.5 percent). This very simple hypothesis allows us to take account of the burden of foreign-debt accumulation.

The Results

The resulting estimated average rates of growth of TFP, capital stock, and output (GDP) during the catch-up period are reported in Table 5. The catch-up period is defined as the number of years the Eastern country takes to reach a level of labor productivity approximately equal to 95 percent of that of the reference country.

TABLE 5

ESTIMATED GROWTH RATES OF TOTAL FACTOR PRODUCTIVITY, CAPITAL STOCK, AND GROSS DOMESTIC PRODUCT IN THE EASTERN EUROPEAN COUNTRIES DURING THE CATCH-UP PERIOD

(*average percentage changes at annual rates*)

	Total Factor Productivity	Capital Stock	Gross Domestic Product	Years to Catch Up
Bulgaria	5.9	9.6	9.0	20
Czechoslovakia	6.1	10.3	10.3	18
GDR	6.2	11.0	9.9	14
Hungary	6.0	9.7	9.0	20
Poland	6.1	10.4	9.8	23
Romania	4.5	7.9	7.1	18
USSR	4.5	8.0	9.1	23

Comparing these results with the data reported in Table 4, it can be seen that the hypothesized rates of growth are quite high, sometimes even higher than those recorded by top performers such as Japan, Germany, Italy, and Greece. This is an important result in itself. The present economic performance of Eastern countries is so poor that extremely high growth rates are required to fill the productivity gaps. This is true even if we scale down the ambition of the catch-up process by choosing less demanding counterpart countries than the human-capital indicators warrant and assume a longer catch-up period.

Table 6 shows the estimates of the initial capital-to-output and capital-to-labor ratios and their levels at the end of the catch-up process. These reflect the fact that we have tried as far as possible in our calibration exercise to make the Eastern countries converge toward Western standards in terms of these ratios.

TABLE 6

CAPITAL-TO-LABOR AND CAPITAL-TO-OUTPUT RATIOS

	Capital-to-Labor Ratio [a]		Capital-to-Output Ratio	
	Initial	Final [b]	Initial	Final [b]
Bulgaria	11.1	69.9	2.2	2.5
Czechoslovakia	14.5	78.4	2.3	2.5
GDR	38.1	162.7	2.5	2.9
Hungary	10.8	72.6	2.3	2.6
Poland	8.1	71.0	2.1	2.4
Romania	10.3	39.7	2.1	2.4
USSR	8.6	52.9	2.3	2.9
Memorandum items:				
FRG	128.9	183.4	3.0	3.1
France	100.0	162.3	2.3	2.6
Italy	110.1	158.1	2.7	2.6
Greece	56.3	83.1	3.8	4.5

[a] In thousands of 1989 U.S. dollars.

[b] Data for the reference countries refer to the fifteenth year.

The net-import requirements that emerge at the end of the exercise are reported in Table 7. They show the size of the resource transfer required to bring the Eastern countries toward the productivity levels of the market economies. The trade deficit of the Eastern European countries jumps from \$4.3 to \$53.7 billion in the first year of our simulation and peaks in the ninth year at \$312.3 billion, which represents

TABLE 7

NET-IMPORT REQUIREMENTS OF THE EASTERN EUROPEAN COUNTRIES
(in billions of 1989 U.S. dollars)

Year	BUL	CZE	GDR	HUN	POL	ROM	USSR	Total[a]
1989	-0.9	0.7	-0.5	1.0	-3.0	2.5	-4.1	-4.3
1	-1.8	-3.2	-23.8	-1.5	-6.2	0.3	-16.8	-53.7
2	-3.0	-6.4	-36.7	-3.2	-8.9	-1.7	-25.5	-85.5
3	-4.3	-9.7	-50.0	-5.0	-11.2	-3.7	-35.3	-119.3
4	-5.7	-13.1	-63.1	-6.9	-13.8	-5.5	-49.5	-157.5
5	-7.0	-16.4	-74.5	-8.8	-18.3	-7.2	-71.4	-203.6
6	-8.3	-19.3	-82.7	-10.7	-22.6	-8.5	-93.2	-245.3
7	-9.5	-21.5	-85.9	-12.3	-27.0	-9.2	-114.1	-279.6
8	-10.3	-22.7	-83.2	-13.5	-31.2	-9.3	-132.6	-302.9
9	-10.8	-22.5	-74.3	-14.1	-35.0	-8.6	-147.1	-312.3
10	-10.7	-20.6	-60.3	-13.8	-37.8	-7.1	-155.8	-306.1
11	-10.0	-17.0	-43.1	-12.3	-39.3	-4.8	-156.9	-283.8
12	-8.7	-12.0	-24.6	-10.7	-39.2	-1.8	-148.8	-245.7
13	-6.8	-5.9	-6.6	-7.9	-37.2	1.8	-130.5	-193.2
14	-4.5	0.9	9.6	-4.5	-33.2	5.5	-101.9	-128.1
15	-2.4	6.9	20.7	-1.3	-28.7	8.7	-72.5	-68.6
16	-0.2	12.6	29.2	2.0	-22.7	11.7	-35.7	-3.0
17	2.0	17.8	35.4	5.2	-15.5	14.4	6.9	66.2
18	4.0	22.2	39.8	8.2	-7.7	16.7	53.2	136.4
19	5.7	25.8	42.9	10.8	0.4	18.7	100.9	205.1
20	7.2	28.7	44.9	12.9	8.4	20.2	148.2	270.4
21	8.4	30.8	42.2	14.7	16.0	21.3	193.1	330.7
22	9.4	32.4	47.1	16.1	23.0	22.1	234.6	384.8
23	10.2	33.5	47.8	17.2	29.1	22.7	271.7	432.3
24	10.8	34.3	48.3	18.0	34.5	23.0	304.1	472.9
25	11.2	34.8	48.8	18.5	39.0	23.1	331.6	506.9
26	11.5	35.0	49.1	18.9	42.7	23.1	354.3	534.8

[a] Numbers are rounded and may not add up to totals.

about 16 percent of the estimated GDP of the whole region.[21] Afterward, the trade balance starts to improve. Although economic activity

[21] One may remember that Canada was continuously in deficit in the nearly half century between 1870 and 1916 for amounts ranging between 2 and 18 percent of GDP and averaging about 7.1 percent (Urquhart, 1986, table 2.11).

continues to grow at brisk rates, investment requirements continue to decline because the productivity gaps are narrowing, and consumption is still hampered by the burden of foreign debt. After the sixteenth year, the Eastern region starts to run trade surpluses with the industrial countries. As we move forward in time, of course, our assumptions become less plausible, particularly our assumption about the constant propensity to consume out of GNP. The most appealing way to get plausible results in the very long run would be to devise a plausible steady state and then let the Eastern countries' "models" move gradually toward it. We have not followed this line of analysis, however, because we are mainly interested in developments during the catch-up period and in its aftermath. The data for the final years of our simulations should, therefore, not be taken very seriously.

As a result of the net-import requirements reported in Table 7 and the corresponding factor-service payments, the Eastern countries rapidly accumulate a large stock of external liabilities (Figure 4).[22] After five years, this stock increases by a factor of about six, from $123.4 to $813.8 billion. External liabilities keep on growing until the nineteenth year of the simulation, when the current account of the whole region moves into surplus. During this period, Eastern countries record striking levels of external liabilities relative to GDP. The peaks are 60 percent of GDP for Romania, 100 percent for the Soviet Union, 127 percent for Czechoslovakia, 164 percent for Bulgaria, 167 percent for Poland, 169 percent for Hungary, and 202 percent for the GDR.[23] In the long run, however, the current-account surpluses recorded by the Eastern countries allow them to improve their external positions; the stock of liabilities falls to about $1,160 billion after the thirtieth year, equivalent to about 17 percent of their aggregate income.

It may be useful to compare our present estimates of Eastern countries' import requirements with those obtained by other authors and those reported by us in a previous version of this paper. The OECD (1990d) carries out an exercise very similar to ours but does not include the GDR or the Soviet Union. In what is considered the optimistic scenario, in which there is a substantial improvement in the economic performance

[22] The term "external liabilities" includes both debt and the stock of foreign direct investment into the Eastern countries.

[23] Given the broad definition of "external liabilities" above, these ratios are not comparable to the debt-to-GDP ratios as usually measured, particularly in the case of indebted less developed countries.

FIGURE 4

PROJECTION OF EXTERNAL LIABILITIES
(in billions of U.S. dollars at five-year intervals)

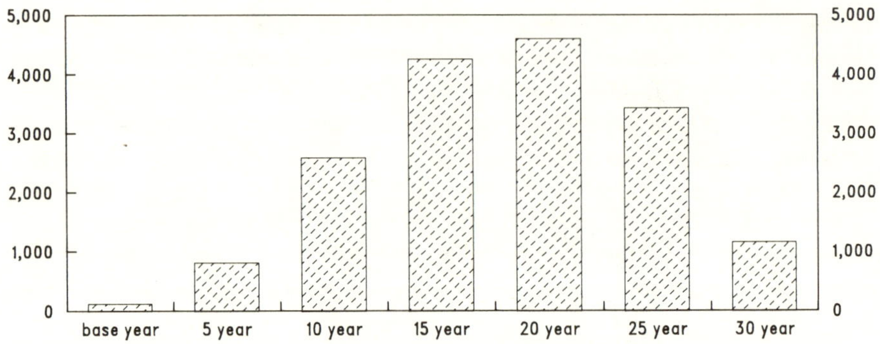

of the Eastern countries,[24] total net imports for the period from 1991 to 1995 are expected to amount to about $221 billion,[25] which is almost equal to our estimate of $229 billion between the second and the sixth year of our simulation.[26] The CEPR estimates (1990), referring to the whole of Eastern Europe except the Soviet Union, are presented as a range; the lower bound, for a ten-year period, is $1,350 billion, and the higher bound is close to $3,000 billion. Our corresponding estimate ($1,224 billion) is below their lower bound. A comparison with Phelps and Fitoussi (1990) is very difficult owing to the different nature of the exercise, but a rough comparison of our estimates with those they present for the aggregate excluding the USSR does not reveal large inconsistencies.

[24] In this case, it is assumed that Hungary and Czechoslovakia reach the same level of output and capital stock per capita as Austria in twenty-five years and that Poland, Bulgaria, and Romania grow at average rates of about 5.0, 2.7, and 2.3 percent, respectively.

[25] The values are originally expressed in deutsche marks at 1990 prices. The dollar figures are calculated by expressing the data in deutsche marks at 1989 prices and then converting them into U.S. dollars at the average exchange rate for that year.

[26] Import requirements are similar, even though the hypothesized rates of economic growth are higher in our simulations. This may be due to different assumptions regarding the initial level of the TFP and its rate of growth.

For the specific case of German unification, the OECD estimates of the GDR's net-import requirements in the first five years after unification are similar to ours when the catch-up period is set at fifteen years. By contrast, Masson and Meredith (1990) obtain figures significantly lower than ours. They consider two scenarios. In the more optimistic scenario, output per worker in the eastern region of Germany is expected to reach 80 percent of the level in the western region by 2001. In the less optimistic scenario, it reaches only 60 percent. The cumulative additional demand on world saving after twelve years is projected to be $452 and $536 billion in the two scenarios, whereas our estimate for the first twelve years is $702 billion.[27]

The estimates we presented in a previous version of this essay were much larger than those given here, ranging from $310 billion in the first year of the simulation to nearly $800 billion at the peak reached in the twenty-second year. The differences between our old estimates and the present ones are due basically to three factors. First, we have reduced the level of catch-up from 100 percent to 95 percent and have lengthened the catch-up period by seven years for Bulgaria, five for Hungary, three for Czechoslovakia and Romania, two for Poland and the USSR, and one for the GDR. Second, we have drastically downgraded the target for the USSR, because we have used a much lower estimate of initial GDP. For example, the USSR was earlier assumed to reach an average counterpart country made up of France, Italy, Spain, and Portugal in twenty-two years, starting from a GDP of $1,564 billion; it is now estimated to reach an average based on Greece and Portugal in twenty-three years, starting from a GDP level of $516 billion. Third, we have assumed in this essay that catch-up will proceed smoothly rather than linearly as in our previous exercise.

All in all, the comparisons with other studies show that our estimates of the net imports required to stimulate catch-up in the Eastern European countries are on the low side. This conclusion should be borne in mind when examining the results reported in the following section.

4 Macroeconomic Effects in the West of Reform in the East

It is reasonable to expect that the bulk of the additional demand of the Eastern European countries will be met by Western economies, which

[27] The figures are originally expressed in billions of U.S. dollars at 1990 prices. We have converted them to 1989 prices by using the percentage change in the GNP deflator in 1990.

can supply the technical and financial resources necessary to foster economic growth. Hence, we have assumed that the net-import requirements of the Eastern economies impinge entirely on the industrial countries.

No precise assumption is needed in this essay regarding the nature of the capital flows financing the large current-account deficits of the Eastern economies during the catch-up process. In the real world, however, the success of the transformation process will depend on the greater part of the financing being provided by foreign direct investment attracted by the higher return on capital. Official financing, from international financial institutions such as the International Monetary Fund, the World Bank, and the European Bank for Reconstruction and Development, can act only as catalyst in this process.

To distribute the additional net exports among the G-8 countries (the G-7 plus an aggregate made up of the remaining small industrial countries, dubbed "Small"), we used a trade matrix for the 1987-1989 period, reflecting the exports of each of the eight Western countries to each of the seven Eastern countries. The additional net exports of each G-8 country shown in Table 8 thus result from combining the import requirement of each Eastern country with the historical bilateral trade pattern.[28] Table 8 shows a very uneven distribution of additional export requirements. Germany and the small industrialized countries have to provide by far the largest amounts of additional resources (about $100 billion at the peak), whereas the United States and the United Kingdom, with a traditionally low level of exports to Eastern European countries, are virtually untouched. The remaining countries are in an intermediate position, although Japan's demand shock is fairly small relative to its economic size.

To assess the potential repercussions on the Western economies, the estimated shocks were imparted to the exports of the G-8 countries using the INTERMOD world model. The exercise is analogous to those carried out, for East Germany alone, by the OECD (1990a) and Masson and Meredith (1990).[29]

Because the export equation in INTERMOD is expressed in terms of the share of the relevant country in world trade, the shock has to take

[28] An analogous exercise to estimate the new direction of trade of Eastern economies was carried out by Collins and Rodrik (1991) looking at the trade flows of "comparable" Western countries and at the pre-war experience. Their final results are similar to ours.

[29] INTERMOD allows for either forward- or backward-looking simulations. We use the former to obtain the results presented below.

TABLE 8

ADDITIONAL NET EXPORTS OF THE G-8 COUNTRIES
(in billions of 1989 U.S. dollars)

Year	CAN	USA	JAP	FRG	FRA	UK	ITA	SMALL
1989	0.3	0.1	0.5	1.2	0.2	0.2	0.4	1.4
1	2.9	0.7	3.0	21.6	3.7	2.1	3.7	16.0
2	4.6	1.2	4.7	34.2	5.9	3.3	5.8	25.6
3	6.6	1.7	6.6	47.5	8.3	4.7	8.2	35.8
4	9.0	2.3	8.9	61.7	10.9	6.3	10.9	47.5
5	12.4	3.2	12.2	77.3	14.2	8.2	14.5	61.7
6	15.6	4.0	15.5	90.7	17.1	9.9	17.8	74.8
7	18.6	4.7	18.4	100.6	19.5	11.4	20.7	85.7
8	21.1	5.3	20.8	105.8	21.1	12.5	22.9	93.5
9	22.8	5.6	22.5	105.4	21.7	13.0	24.2	97.1
10	23.5	5.7	23.2	99.3	21.2	12.9	24.3	96.0
11	22.9	5.5	22.7	87.8	19.7	12.1	23.2	89.7
12	21.1	5.0	21.0	71.6	17.0	10.6	20.8	78.5
13	17.8	4.1	17.9	52.1	13.3	8.5	17.0	62.4
14	13.2	3.0	13.4	29.8	8.8	5.7	12.1	42.3
15	8.6	1.8	9.0	10.6	4.6	3.2	7.3	23.5
16	3.1	0.5	3.7	-9.3	0	0.3	1.9	2.7
17	-3.0	-1.0	-2.2	-29.1	-4.9	-2.7	-3.9	-19.4
18	-9.4	-2.6	-8.5	-48.4	-9.8	-5.7	-10.0	-41.9
19	-15.9	-4.2	-14.9	-66.7	-14.7	-8.7	-16.0	-64.0
20	-22.3	-5.7	-21.2	-83.7	-19.3	-11.5	-21.8	-85.0
21	-28.3	-7.1	-27.1	-99.0	-23.5	-14.1	-27.2	-104.4
22	-33.7	-8.5	-32.5	-112.5	-27.3	-16.4	-32.0	-121.8
23	-38.6	-9.6	-37.3	-124.3	-30.7	-18.4	-36.3	-137.1
24	-42.7	-10.6	-41.5	-134.2	-33.6	-20.1	-39.9	-150.2
25	-46.2	-11.5	-45.0	-142.5	-36.0	-21.5	-43.0	-161.2
26	-49.1	-12.2	-47.9	-149.3	-37.9	-22.7	-45.5	-170.1

the same form. In a way, all G-8 countries are assumed to gain market share. This occurs because they increase their exports to the Eastern countries, which are outside the model. As has already been emphasized, the shock is particularly large. In the cases of Germany and the small industrialized countries, it corresponds to a 5 percentage point increase in the country's share of world exports when the demand shock reaches its peak in the thirteenth year. For Canada, Italy, Japan, and France, it corresponds to a 1 to 1.5 percentage point gain in market share. The shock is smaller for the United Kingdom (0.8 percent) and United States (0.4 percent) because of their small trade linkages with Eastern countries.

The results, expressed in terms of deviations from the baseline, show that it would be utterly undesirable from a macroeconomic point of view for such a huge demand shock to hit the Western economies. The effects on interest and exchange rates would be disruptive. In the seventh or eighth year of the simulation, when the shock wave reaches its acme, long-run real interest rates increase by a minimum of 2.4 percent in the United States and a maximum of 4.5 percent in Germany (Figure 5); the rise for the weighted average of the G-8 countries is about 3 percent at the peak. The decrease in the trade deficits of the Eastern countries in the following years and the eventual emergence of the sizable surpluses, bring about a gradual reduction of real interest rates, which return to their baseline level before the twentieth year and then fall about two points below it.

FIGURE 5

EXPORT SHOCK: LONG-RUN REAL INTEREST RATES

(percentage point deviations from the baseline)

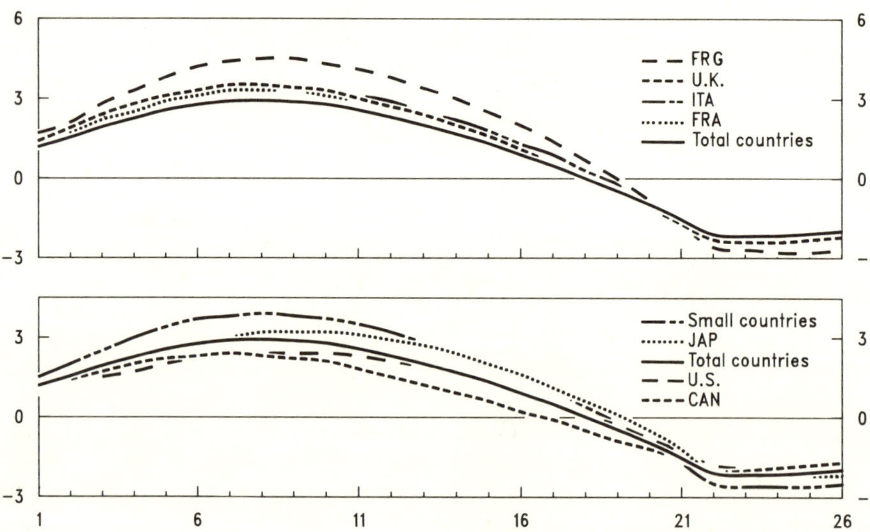

As regards exchange rates, the estimates (reflecting the forward-looking nature of INTERMOD) show a sharp-impact appreciation of the deutsche mark against the U.S. dollar by 20 percent; the currency of the small industrialized countries appreciates by about 12 percent and that of Canada by 6 percent; the lira, French franc, and British pound rise by about 8 percent, and the yen appreciates by 3 percent (Figure 6). The various currencies then depreciate gradually against the dollar and go back to the baseline level, which, with the exception of the yen, they reach between the thirteenth and the fourteenth year. Subsequently, they continue to lose value gradually, depreciating eventually by an amount approximately equal to the initial appreciation. Such exchange-rate fluctuations would greatly strain the stability of the European Monetary System (EMS). In fact, although the currencies of the United Kingdom, France, and Italy stay very close together and that of the small industrialized countries follows a fairly similar path, the initial wide appreciation of the deutsche mark followed by an equal depreciation seems incompatible with exchange-rate fixity.

FIGURE 6

EXPORT SHOCK: NOMINAL EXCHANGE RATES VS. THE U.S. DOLLAR
(percentage point deviations from the baseline)

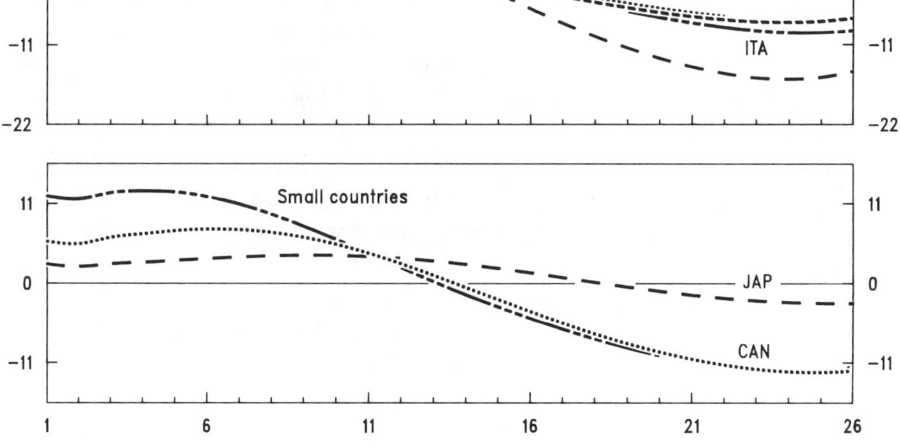

Part of our result reflects the fact that we have kept the western and eastern regions of Germany separate, each with its own currency. One might approximate the macroeconomic variables for unified Germany by taking a weighted average of those for the two German regions, but this rough approach is difficult to apply to the exchange rate. Had we been able to extend our exercise to East Germany, it is obvious that its currency would have depreciated. It is very difficult, however, to assess the extent to which this would have offset the appreciation of the deutsche mark. The only way to gauge the result of these two opposite forces is to look at the trade balance of a unified Germany, obtained by summing the balances of the GDR and FRG (Tables 7 and 8). The aggregate balance is slightly negative in the first five years of the simulation, swings into significant surplus for twelve years, for a cumulative total of about $350 billion, and then returns to deficits. In the first seventeen years, the positive shock to the trade balance of a unified Germany is significantly larger than that recorded by Italy but much smaller than that registered by the small industrialized countries (Table 8). Even if the strength of the deutsche mark is diminished by the weight of reconstruction in the eastern region of Germany, exchange-rate tensions in Europe cannot be excluded, because of the huge transfer of resources implied by the reconstruction needs of Eastern Europe as a whole.

The large increase of interest rates and, in all countries except the United States, the appreciation of the currency cannot prevent serious inflationary pressures. In the eleventh year, the German GNP deflator is about 13 percent higher than in the baseline, corresponding to an additional average yearly rate of inflation exceeding 1 percent, notwithstanding an unchanged money supply (Figure 7). Around the same date, the GNP deflators are about 9 percent above baseline in Canada, France, the United Kingdom, Italy, and the small industrialized countries, and 6 percent above baseline in the United States and Japan. In Germany in some years, the increase of the inflation rate reaches 2 percent.

Output prices return to the baseline level around the twentieth year of the simulation and then decrease quite significantly because of the deflation brought about by the increasing trade surplus of the Eastern countries. The last few years of the simulation should not, as argued above, be given too much weight, but the pattern of inflationary tensions, initially, and deflationary impulses, subsequently, are indicative of the disturbances inflicted on the Western economies.

FIGURE 7

EXPORT SHOCK: GROSS NATIONAL PRODUCT DEFLATORS

(percentage point deviations from the baseline)

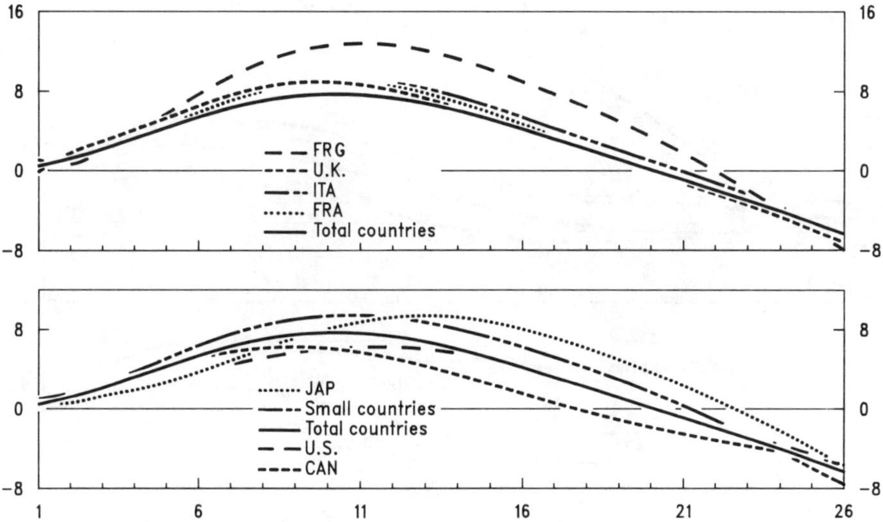

The same message is conveyed by the behavior of GNP (Figure 8). For the aggregate of the G-8 countries, there is little if any change for the first ten years and a small gain thereafter, amounting to about 2 percent by the twentieth year. This reflects the positive effect of the reform process in the Eastern countries, which increases world efficiency in the long run. For Germany, however, there is a 2-percent loss in the first two years, caused by the jump in the exchange rate and interest rate brought about by the forward-looking nature of the macro model used. In subsequent years, however, there is a gain in national income resulting from the increased export demand and, subsequently, from the earnings on the increasing net-foreign-asset position. Around the twentieth year of the simulation, West German GNP is about 5.5 percent higher than in the baseline. The pattern is similar but less pronounced for the small industrialized countries, while little happens in the remaining countries. Nevertheless, the sizable crowding-out of domestic demand (especially investment) causes GDP to develop much less favorably than GNP, and, in all the G-8 countries, domestic income is below baseline in the thirteenth year.

FIGURE 8

EXPORT SHOCK: GROSS NATIONAL PRODUCT

(percentage point deviations from the baseline)

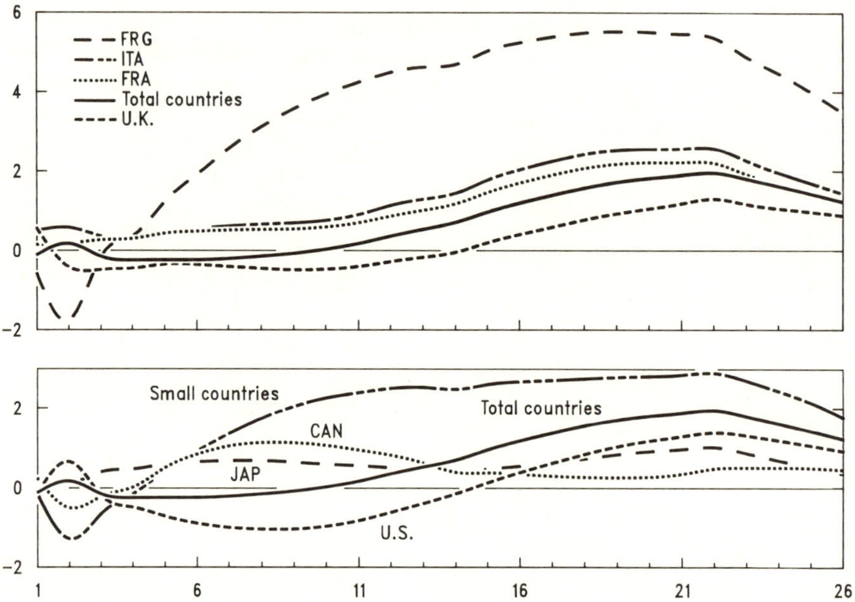

5 The Case of an Offsetting Fiscal Action in the Western Countries

The obvious line of defence for a country confronted with an excess of demand is to resort to fiscal policy by reducing government expenditures (which is also the exogenous budget variable in INTERMOD). To do this, we have assumed that government expenditures are changed annually by an amount equal to half the net-export shock (that is, the figures reported in Table 8 above).

The results of the simulation with this fiscal offset are much more tolerable. The long-run real rate of interest now increases by only 1 percentage point in Germany in the fifth year of the simulation, when the peak is reached, and by half a percentage point or less in the other countries (Figure 9). Under the simple fiscal-policy rule we have adopted, however, there are large swings in real interest rates in the later years of the simulation, when the fiscal stimulus offsetting the trade of Western countries is evidently too large. The important message, however, is conveyed by the first part of the simulation, when the fiscal offset significantly reduces tensions. The deutsche mark now jumps by only 9 percent with respect to the dollar in the first year, followed by the "currency" of the small industrialized countries at 5 percent, while all the other currencies, except the yen, appreciate by around 3 percent (Figure 10). Around the thirteenth year, the appreciation of the various currencies against the dollar is reduced to about 1 percent. Bearing in mind the remarks made above about the need to scale down the simulated appreciation of the deutsche mark to reflect the offsetting influence of the reconstruction needs of East Germany, there is no evidence that exchange-rate movements would be inconsistent with the constraints imposed by the EMS and with the irrevocably fixed rates envisaged to achieve European Economic and Monetary Union (EMU).

The results are also less worrisome with regard to inflation. The increase in the average yearly rate of inflation in Germany is less than three-tenths of 1 percent by the ninth year of the simulation, and it is smaller still in the other G-8 countries (Figure 11). Indeed, except for the end of the period, when our rough fiscal-policy rule gives excessive fiscal stimulus, the price level is close to the baseline value. The behavior of GNP is also more acceptable because there are gains with respect to the baseline in all countries (Figure 12). The changes are not significant for the United States, Japan, and the United Kingdom, but they reach 4 and 3 percent for Germany and Canada by the fifteenth year, equivalent to two- or three-tenths of 1 percent per year on average. The gain consists mainly of the income on net foreign assets; in fact, consumption and investment tend to decrease in the initial years of the simulation, crowded out by higher real interest rates, and GDP is significantly lower than GNP.

To achieve a fiscal offset of the size assumed above, government expenditures must be reduced with respect to the baseline; they must fall by a maximum of about 25 percent in Germany around the ninth year of the simulation and by 10 to 20 percent in Canada, France, Italy, and the small industrialized countries, but by much smaller amounts in the United States, Japan, and the United Kingdom. The required cuts are very large for the continental European countries, underlining the incisiveness of the measures required to free the resources necessary to reconstruct the Eastern economies while avoiding strains in the Western industrial economies.

More generally, the results discussed above are at the limit of what is acceptable in terms of macroeconomic consequences. Three factors could push the macroeconomic results beyond that limit. First, any attempt by the Eastern countries to achieve more ambitious results,

FIGURE 9

EXPORT SHOCK WITH GOVERNMENT EXPENDITURE ADJUSTMENT: LONG-RUN REAL INTEREST RATES

(percentage point deviations from the baseline)

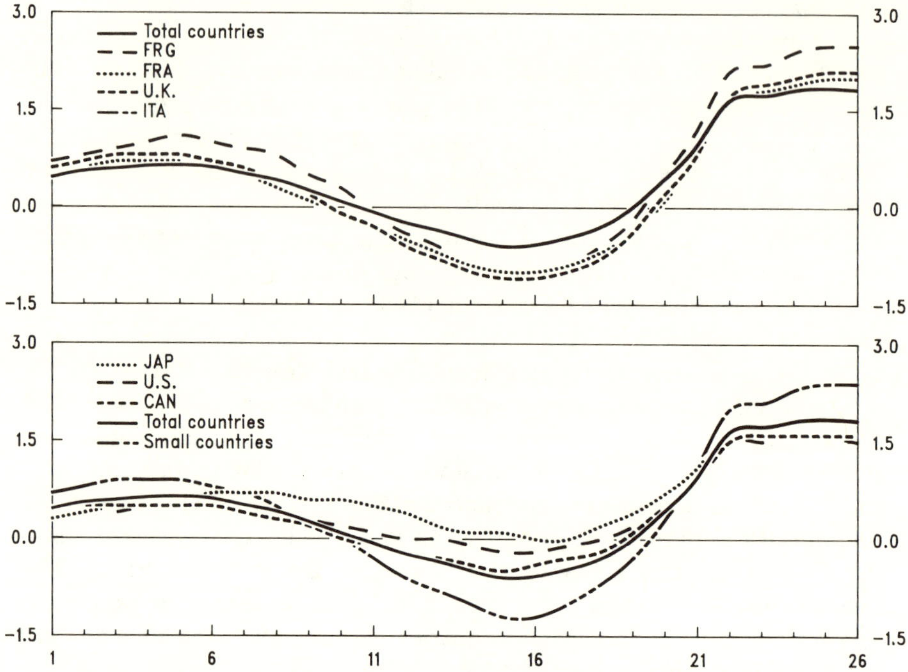

NOTE: Italy overlaps the line for France in the first twelve years and the line for the United Kingdom thereafter.

FIGURE 10

EXPORT SHOCK WITH GOVERNMENT EXPENDITURE ADJUSTMENT: NOMINAL EXCHANGE RATES VS. THE U.S. DOLLAR

(percentage point deviations from the baseline)

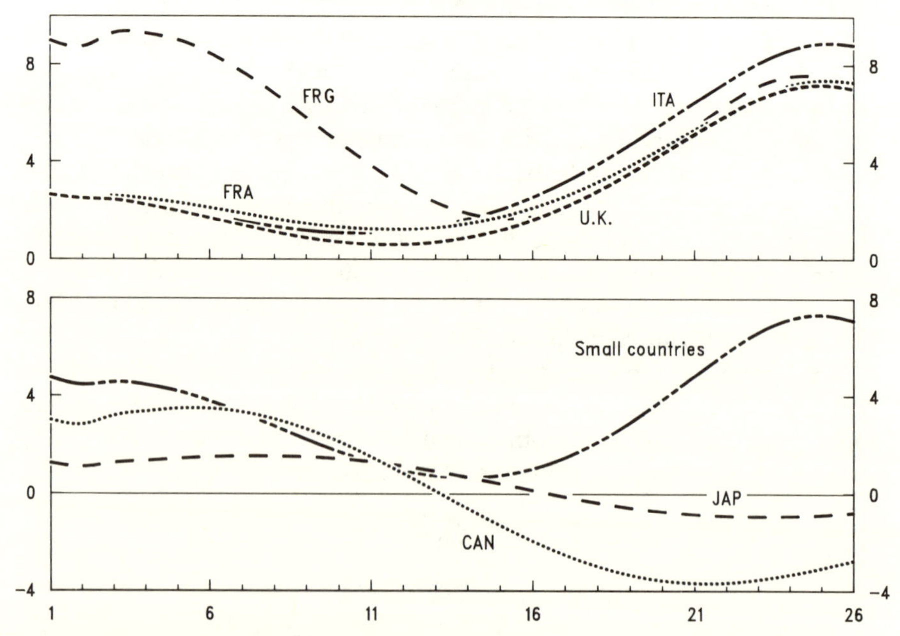

FIGURE 11

EXPORT SHOCK WITH GOVERNMENT EXPENDITURE ADJUSTMENT: GROSS NATIONAL PRODUCT DEFLATORS

(percentage point deviations from the baseline)

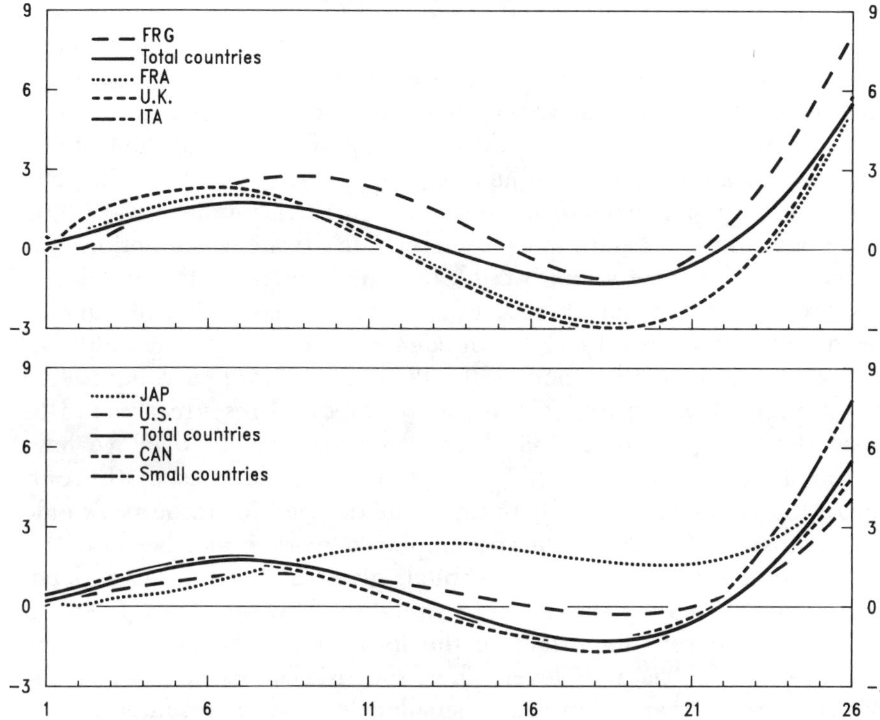

FIGURE 12

EXPORT SHOCK WITH GOVERNMENT EXPENDITURE ADJUSTMENT: GROSS NATIONAL PRODUCT

(percentage point deviations from the baseline)

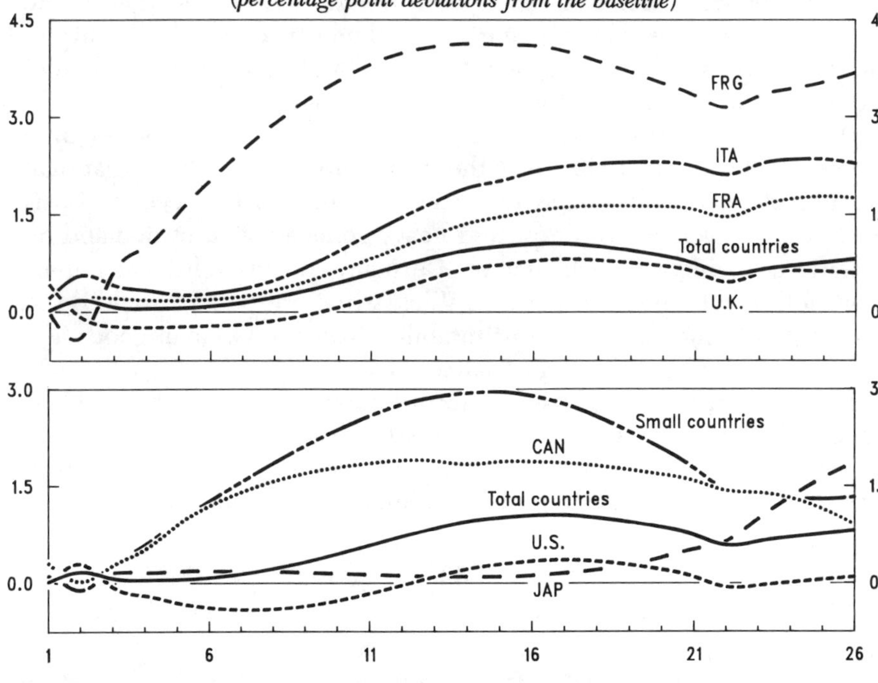

either by shortening the period in which the catch-up is completed or by aiming at higher income levels, would be frustrated by the inability of the industrial countries to provide the necessary resources, whatever the macroeconomic policies pursued. Second, our simulations have assumed that, notwithstanding the loosening of the grip of the state on income distribution and accumulation, the Eastern countries manage to maintain very high rates of national saving, which implies a very tight fiscal policy to offset the expected increase in private consumption. Any reduction in national saving would, of course, increase the amount of resources needed from abroad. For instance, a reduction of national saving by 1 percent in the Eastern countries would increase additional import requirements by about $20 billion in the ninth year, equivalent to 6.5 percent of the total. Third, more imported resources would be needed if the pace of technical progress were slower than we have assumed in our simulations. In the setting we have used, the only factor that could substantially mitigate the demand for resources would be a substantial decrease in the employed work force, because this would reduce the demand for capital, given a target level of labor productivity. Apart from its undesirability, however, this factor is unlikely to be very important in the long run, when unemployment should be at its "natural" level. Thus, the risk factors lie more in the direction of a larger rather than a smaller demand for resources.

It is therefore useful to ask what other lines of defence the Western economies could adopt if the demand for resources were larger than envisaged. Monetary policy is not an answer. It could only assume a more restrictive stance in order to fight inflation, thus exacerbating the rise in interest rates, the crowding out of domestic demand and output, and the dispersion of exchange rates. Structural policy is the only tool left, and it has a very precise meaning in this setting.

Our exercise throws into full relief one aspect already noted by a recent CEPR study (1990): that the problem posed by the gargantuan amount of resources needed to reconstruct the Eastern economies is made more severe by the expected heavy concentration of demand on specific countries, in particular on Germany, if the additional import flows follow the historical pattern. What structural policy should do in this case is to increase the substitutability between German goods and those produced by other industrial countries.

To a certain extent, of course, substitutability is not determined by policies but by the intrinsic characteristics of goods and other natural factors such as geographical propinquity. Trade policies, however, may introduce an artificial degree of differentiation. Consider, for example, procurement policies that administratively prefer national goods over foreign goods, or protectionist agricultural policies that treat domestically produced goods very differently from those produced abroad. Comprehensive trade liberalization is the obvious structural policy to help spread the additional demand of Eastern countries toward the United States, Japan, and the United Kingdom. Examples include the implementation of the Single Market at the European level and a successful final outcome of the Uruguay Round at the world level. The favorable effect of such moves would be enhanced by the efficiency gains, discussed by Cecchini (1988) and Baldwin (1989a), which increase available resources. Structural moves of this kind would spread the gains from increased productivity in the East more evenly across the industrialized countries while easing the strains on exchange rates and the differentiated behavior of real interest rates and prices.

6 Concluding Remarks

With all the caveats that necessarily accompany an exercise like ours, and remembering the specific assumptions on which it is built, the most interesting conclusions that emerge from our study are:

(1) If the economies of Central and Eastern Europe are to develop the full potential warranted by their endowments of human capital and to catch up to their Western counterparts, they will need, in addition to very deep and difficult structural reforms, resource transfers on a scale that will cause substantial and sustained current-account deficits, on a level reminiscent of the Canadian experience at the turn of the century.

(2) If the Western industrialized countries are called upon to complement (essentially through direct investment) national saving in the Eastern countries to finance Eastern economic reconstruction, the consequences will be unbearable in terms of interest-rate increases, exchange-rate changes, inflation, and the crowding out of local production, accompanied by unemployment. Only in the very long run, will there be favorable effects from the substantial increase in the income on foreign assets. By increasing national saving in the West, however, an incisive tightening of fiscal policies could mitigate the negative consequences while leaving the favorable effects substantially unchanged.

(3) There are grounds for fearing that the demand for resources to reconstruct the Eastern economies could be even larger than estimated in this essay. The policy actions necessary to counteract the unfavorable effects of such an outcome include (a) readiness to increase the national saving rate in the East, by reducing public expenditure if

necessary, and (b) incisive trade liberalization to reduce the artificial differentiation of the products of the various industrial countries so as to spread the demand shock originating in the East more evenly among the Western countries.

7 Appendix: Investment Inefficiency, Reforms, and Economic Growth

What is particularly striking in comparing the Eastern and Western European economies is the association in the East of high rates of investment with low rates of output growth. As has been stressed by the OECD (1990b, p. 48), this evidence suggests that "much investment has been largely wasted, so that the effective, potentially productive capital stock is small in relation to the cumulative investment effort undertaken." In this Appendix, we present a simple growth model by means of which we try to illustrate conceptually the consequences of the existence and removal of inefficiency in investment.[30] In highly simplified and abstract terms, the model shows what basic factors are at work when reform takes place in the East, and it can be regarded as the conceptual framework for our empirical work.[31]

We assume that the world economy consists of two countries, a representative Western country and a representative Eastern country. For simplicity, we make the heroic assumption that the two countries are identical in every respect except investment efficiency.[32] In particular,

[30] The fundamental reasons for this inefficiency have been emphasized by the United Nations Economic Commission for Europe (1990, pp. 1-6):

> Lead times are long and have tended to increase in the 1980s (that is, the proportion of unfinished, non-performing investment projects in gross fixed investment has risen), the latter is partly due to a systematic tendency for enterprises to start an excessive number of new investment projects in order to get them "into the plan" and so lay a claim on future investment funds; equipment is often out of date by the time it is actually installed and operating; there appear to be widespread co-ordination failures in balancing supplies of labor, material inputs and productive capacities, and material and energy consumption per unit of output is very high in comparison with market economies, in part owing to a structural bias in the development process which favored the nurturing of the upstream sectors of "heavy" industry, but also reflecting generally lower levels of efficiency and technology throughout the productive process.

[31] The one sector model we present below cannot, by definition, capture the wrong allocation of resources among sectors, another source of inefficiency in the East.

[32] The structure of the model, however, would allow for considerable differences in other critical parameters.

we assume that investment in the Eastern country does not translate entirely into capital accumulation; part of it is wasted as a result of the distortions present in the economy.[33] As in Lipton and Sachs (1983), saving behavior is not determined by *ad hoc* assumptions, as, for example, by making saving proportional to disposable income or wealth (see Fischer and Frenkel, 1974a, 1974b; Oniki and Uzawa, 1965; and Ruffin, 1979); it is obtained from the intertemporal maximizing behavior of individuals. Following Svensson and Razin (1982), individuals are simultaneously consumers and investors, and they choose investment to maximize their wealth, defined as the present value of net output. Because the two economies are linked together by an international commodity and capital market and they produce a single, identical good that can be either consumed or used for capital accumulation, the present model can be defined as a "pure-absorption" model.[34] We also assume that the world has a life span of two periods.

Buiter (1981) uses an overlapping-generations setting similar to ours to explain international capital movements in terms of different rates of time preference in the two countries. In our model, the critical determinant of international trade and of international capital movements is the presence of investment inefficiency in the Eastern country.

The Model

In both the Western and the Eastern country, output (Q) is given by a Cobb-Douglas production function. There are only two productive factors, capital (K) and labor (L). In each country, labor is equal to the population, which is assumed to be constant and therefore normalized to one. Therefore, we can write

$$q_t = k_t^{\alpha}, \qquad t = 1, 2 \tag{A.1}$$

$$q_t^* = k_t^{*\alpha}, \qquad t = 1, 2, \tag{A.1'}$$

in which all the variables are expressed in per capita terms, α is the

[33] This hypothesis resembles that of the costs of installing investment goods adopted by, for example, Tobin (1969), Abel (1981), and Lipton and Sachs (1983).

[34] Buiter (1981, p. 779) stressed that "international trade and international lending and borrowing (international capital mobility) are part and parcel of the same transaction. In a one-commodity model, the only way to pay for an extra unit of output today is with a promise of future output. Each trade balance transaction has to involve credit."

elasticity of output with respect to capital, and t is the time index. All variables associated with the Eastern country are marked by an asterisk.

Individuals in both countries maximize identical logarithmic utility functions subject to present-value budget constraints:

$$\begin{aligned} \max U &= \ln c_1 + \left(\frac{1}{1+\theta}\right) \ln c_2 \\ \text{st } c_1 &+ \left(\frac{1}{1+r}\right) c_2 = W \end{aligned} \tag{A.2}$$

$$\begin{aligned} \max U^* &= \ln c_1^* + \left(\frac{1}{1+\theta}\right) \ln c_2^* \\ \text{st } c_1^* &+ \left(\frac{1}{1+r}\right) c_2^* = W^* , \end{aligned} \tag{A.2'}$$

in which c_t is consumption at time t, θ is the (constant) rate of time preference, r is the world interest rate, and W is the country's wealth. Wealth is defined as the present value of future net output (that is, gross output minus investment):

$$W = \left(q_1 - i_1\right) + \left(\frac{1}{1+r}\right) q_2 \tag{A.3}$$

$$W^* = \left(q_1^* - i_1^*\right) + \left(\frac{1}{1+r}\right) q_2^* , \tag{A.3'}$$

in which i denotes investment. We assume that capital depreciates entirely during the productive process so that investment in the first period corresponds to the capital stock in the second period (obviously, in the second and final period, investment is nil). As to first-period investment, we have

$$i_1 = k_2 \tag{A.4}$$

$$i_1^* = \left(1 + z^*\right) k_2^* , \qquad z^* > 0 , \tag{A.4'}$$

in which z^* is the inefficiency factor affecting investment in the Eastern country. In that country, it takes $1 + z^*$ units of output to increase the capital stock by one unit, because of waste during the investment process.

The model is closed by the commodity-market equilibrium condition

$$q_t + q_t^* = c_t + c_t^* + i_t + i_t^* , \qquad t = 1, 2 . \tag{A.5}$$

In summary, the problem is to choose consumption in the two periods and investment, or more precisely the capital stock, in the second period, so as to maximize the intertemporal utility function.

Properties of the Model

Choosing the second-period capital stock so as to maximize wealth yields

$$\alpha k_2^{-(1-\alpha)} = 1 + r \tag{A.6}$$

$$\frac{\alpha k_2^{*\,-(1-\alpha)}}{1 + z^*} = 1 + r . \tag{A.6'}$$

The left-hand side of equations (A.6) and (A.6′) is the marginal productivity of capital in the second period. Because z^* is greater than zero, the second-period capital stock is lower in the Eastern country than in the Western country:

$$k_2 = \left[\frac{\alpha}{1 + r}\right]^{\frac{1}{1-\alpha}} \tag{A.7}$$

$$k_2^* = \left[\frac{\alpha}{(1 + z^*)(1 + r)}\right]^{\frac{1}{1-\alpha}} . \tag{A.7'}$$

The second-period capital stock is an inverse function of the world interest rate and, in the case of the Eastern country, of the investment-inefficiency parameter.

Plugging investment into the budget constraint and performing the constrained maximization of the utility function, we determine consumption in periods one and two for each country:

$$c_1 = \left(\frac{1+\theta}{2+\theta}\right)\left[q_1 + \left(\frac{1-\alpha}{\alpha}\right)k_2\right]$$
$$c_2 = \left(\frac{1+r}{1+\theta}\right)c_1 \tag{A.8}$$

$$c_1^* = \left(\frac{1+\theta}{2+\theta}\right)\left[q_1^* + \left(\frac{1-\alpha}{\alpha}\right)(1+z^*)k_2^*\right]$$
$$c_2^* = \left(\frac{1+r}{1+\theta}\right)c_1^* \,. \tag{A.8$'$}$$

The world interest rate is determined by the commodity-market equilibrium condition (equation A.5 at time 1), which states that world saving is equal to world investment. Hence, "the world pool of savings is channeled to profitable investment projects without regard to the national origin of the savings" (Lipton and Sachs, 1983, p. 138). Making the necessary substitutions, we obtain

$$r = \alpha\left(\frac{\Omega Z}{\Lambda}\right)^{1-\alpha} - 1 \,, \tag{A.9}$$

in which

$$\Omega = \frac{1+\alpha+\theta}{\alpha} \,,$$

$$Z = 1 + \left(\frac{1}{1+z^*}\right)^{\frac{\alpha}{1-\alpha}} \,, \text{ and}$$

$$\Lambda = q_1 + q_1^* \,.$$

It is possible to demonstrate that the derivative of r with respect to z^* is negative and that the elasticity is less than one. Therefore, we can write

$$r = \rho(z^*) \,, \quad \rho'(\cdot) < 0 \,, \quad \eta_{r,z^*} < 1 \,. \tag{A.10}$$

Thus, given the first-period factor endowment and the value of the inefficiency parameter, the model determines simultaneously the world interest rate, the two countries' consumption, investment, and production, and the trade balance in the first and second periods.

If we assume that the first-period capital endowment is lower in the Eastern than in the Western economy, it is possible to demonstrate that the Eastern economy will be characterized by (1) a lower level of output and consumption in both periods, (2) a higher share of investment relative to its output level, and (3) a trade deficit in the first period (which will be equal to the current-account deficit because we have assumed that the initial level of foreign debt is nil).

Now suppose that the implementation of market-oriented reforms in the Eastern country wipes out the investment inefficiency. Investment in the East will be stimulated because the optimal second-period capital stock increases. This, in turn, produces an excess of world investment over world saving that will lead to an increase in the world interest rate.

In the Western country, households are therefore induced to postpone consumption in order to smooth spending over the two periods as the increase in the world interest rate will reduce the second-period capital stock and second-period output. Given output in the first period, the resulting rise in saving and the decline in domestic investment improve the trade balance of the Western country in the first period. In fact, Western entrepreneurs carry out direct investment in the Eastern country to take advantage of the higher capital productivity.

In the Eastern country, the increase in the world interest rate will only offset part of the effect on the second-period capital stock of the decline in the investment inefficiency, because η_{r,z^*} is less than 1. It is possible to demonstrate that the resulting growth in investment is partly financed by domestic saving. The rest of the financing will be provided by the Western economy, as we have already pointed out. At the end, the Eastern economy will catch up to the Western economy with respect to output and the capital-to-labor ratio. This will allow the Eastern country to increase the second-period consumption, compared to what it was with the investment inefficiency, notwithstanding the higher debt it must service. The Western country will also increase spending in the second period, even though production will decline compared to its level in the previous case, because of the greater first-period accumulation of foreign assets. In summary, the removal of the investment inefficiency raises world welfare because it moves both countries onto a higher indifference curve.

References

Abel, A., "Dynamic Effects of Permanent and Temporary Tax Policies in a q Model of Investment," *Journal of Monetary Economics*, 9 (No. 3, 1981) pp. 353-373.

Abramovitz, M., "Rapid Growth Potential and its Realisation: The Experience of Capitalist Economies in the Postwar Period," in E. Malinvaud, ed., *Proceedings of the Fifth World Congress of the International Economic Association*, Vol. 1, London, Macmillan, 1979, pp. 1-51.

Alton, T.P., K. Badach, R. Bakondi, E.M. Bass, J.T. Bombelles, A. Brumaru, G. Lazarcik, and G.J. Staller, "Economic Growth in Eastern Europe 1975-1989," Research Project on National Income in East Central Europe, Occasional Paper No. 110, New York, L.W. International Financial Research, 1990.

Baldwin, R., "The Growth Effects of 1992," *Economic Policy*, No. 9 (October 1989a), pp. 247-281.

———, "Measuring 1992's Medium-Term Dynamic Effects," National Bureau of Economic Research Working Paper No. 3166, Cambridge, Mass., National Bureau of Economic Research, November 1989b.

Barro, R.J., and X. Sala i Martin, "Economic Growth and Convergence Across the United States," National Bureau of Economic Research Working Paper No. 3419, Cambridge, Mass., National Bureau of Economic Research, August 1990.

Baumol, W.J., "Productivity Growth, Convergence and Welfare: What the Long-Run Data Show," *The American Economic Review*, 76 (No. 5, 1986), pp. 1072-1085.

Becker, G.S., *Human Capital*, Cambridge, Mass., National Bureau of Economic Research, 1975.

Bergson, A., "Comparative Productivity: The USSR, Eastern Europe, and the West," *The American Economic Review*, 77 (No. 3, 1987), pp. 342-357.

Buiter, W.H., "Time preference and International Lending and Borrowing in an Overlapping-Generations Model," *Journal of Political Economy*, 89 (No. 41, 1981), pp. 769-797.

Burkett, J.P., and B. Skegro, "Capitalism, Socialism, and Productivity: An Econometric Analysis of CES and Translog Functions," *European Economic Review*, 33 (No. 6, 1989), pp. 1115-1133.

Cecchini, P. *The European Challenge 1992: The Benefits of a Single Market*, Brookfield, Vt., Gower, 1988.

Centre for Economic Policy Research (CEPR), *Monitoring European Integration. The Impact of Eastern Europe*, October, London, CEPR, 1990.

Chenery, H., "Growth and Transformation," in H. Chenery, S. Robinson, and M. Syrquin, eds., *Industrialization and Growth: A Comparative Study*, New York, Oxford University Press for the World Bank, 1986, pp. 13-36.

Collins, S.M., and D. Rodrik, *Eastern Europe and the Soviet Union in the World Economy*, Washington, D.C., Institute for International Economics, May 1991.

Denison, E.F., *Why Growth Rates Differ*, Washington, D.C., The Brookings Institution, 1967.

Ellman, M., *Collectivisation, Convergence and Capitalism: Political Economy in a Divided World*, London, Academic Press, 1984.

Englander, S.A., "Tests of Total Factor Productivity Measurement," OECD Working Paper No. 54, Paris, Organisation for Economic Co-operation and Development, June 1988.

Englander, S.A., and A. Mittelstadt, "Total Factor Productivity: Macroeconomic and Structural Aspects of the Slowdown," *OECD Economic Studies*, No. 10 (Spring 1988).

Fischer, S., and J. Frenkel, "Interest Rate Equalization and Patterns of Production, Trade and Consumption in a Two-Country Growth Model," *The Economic Record*, 50 (December 1974a), pp. 555-580.

———, "Economic Growth and Stages of the Balance of Payments: A Theoretical Model," in G. Horwich and P.A. Samuelson, eds., *Trade, Stability, and Macroeconomics: Essays in Honor of Lloyd A. Metzler*, New York, Academic Press, 1974b, pp. 503-521.

Fitoussi, J.P., and E.S. Phelps, "Global Effects of Eastern European Rebuilding and the Adequacy of Western Saving: An Issue for the 1990s," paper presented at the Second Annual Villa Mondragone Conference on World Saving: Prosperity and Growth (Rome, July 1990.

Giustiniani, A., Papadia, F., and D. Porciani, "Gli effetti delle riforme economiche nei paesi dell'est europeo sulle economie industriali occidentali: un approccio macroeconomico," *Rivista di Politica Economica*, 81 (June 1991), pp. 143-188.

Goldsmith, R.W., *Comparative National Balance Sheets*, Chicago and London, The University of Chicago Press, 1985.

Group of Ten (G-10), "Issues Raised by the Transition in Central and Eastern Europe," A Report to the Ministers and Governors by the Chairman of the Group of Deputies, Rome, Group of Ten, April 1991.

Kuznets, S., *Population, Capital, and Growth: Selected Essays*, New York, Norton, 1973.

Larre, B., and R. Torres, "Is Convergence a Spontaneous Process? The Experience of Spain, Portugal and Greece," *OECD Economic Studies*, No. 16 (Spring 1991), pp. 169-198.

Lauterbach, A., "The 'Convergence' Controversy Revisited," *Kyklos*, 29 (Fasc. 4, 1976), pp. 733-754.

Lipschitz, L., and D. McDonald, eds., "German Unification: Economic Issues," Occasional Paper 75, Washington, D.C., International Monetary Fund, December 1990.

Lipton, D., and J. Sachs, "Accumulation and Growth in a Two-Country Model: A Simulation Approach," *Journal of International Economics*, 15 (No. 2, 1983), pp. 135-159.

Lucas, R.E., "On the Mechanics of Economic Development," *Journal of Monetary Economics*, 22 (No. 1, 1988), pp. 3-42.

Maddison, A., "Long Run Dynamics of Productivity Growth," *BNL Quarterly Review*, No. 128 (1979), pp. 3-43.

———, *Phases of Capitalist Development*, Oxford and New York, Oxford University Press, 1982.

———, "Growth and Slowdown in Advanced Capitalist Economies: Techniques of Quantitative Assessment," *Journal of Economic Literature*, 25 (June 1987), pp. 643-698.

Masson, P.R., and G. Meredith, "Domestic and International Macroeconomic Consequences of German Unification," in L. Lipschitz and D. McDonald, eds., "German Unification: Economic Issues," Occasional Paper 75, Washington, D.C., International Monetary Fund, December 1990.

Masson, P.R., S. Symansky, and G. Meredith, "MULTIMOD Mark II: A Revised and Extended Model," Occasional Paper 71, Washington, D.C., International Monetary Fund, July 1990.

Meredith, G., "INTERMOD 2.0: Model Specification and Simulation Properties," Department of Finance, Ottawa, Working Paper No. 89-7, 1989.

Nuti, D.M. (1988), "Perestroika: Transition from Central Planning to Market Socialism," *Economic Policy: A European Forum*, No. 7 (1988), pp. 355-389.

Organisation of Economic Co-operation and Development (OECD), "The Impact of German Economic and Monetary Union in OECD Countries," Note by the Secretariat, Paris, OECD, May 1990a.

———, *OECD Economic Outlook*, 47, Paris, Organisation of Economic Co-operation and Development, June 1990b.

———, "Modelisation des économies planifiées en transition," Note by the Secretariat, DES/CPE/EX(90)3, Paris, Organisation of Economic Co-operation and Development, September 1990c.

———, *Quarterly Labour Force Statistics*, No. 3, Paris, Organisation of Economic Co-operation and Development, September 1990d.

Oniki, H., and Uzawa, "Patterns of Trade and Investment in a Dynamic Model of International Trade," *The Review of Economic Studies*, 32 (January 1965), pp. 15-38.

Papoulis, A., *Probability, Random Variables, and Stochastic Processes*, New York, McGraw-Hill, 1965 (2nd edition 1984).

PlanEcon, *How Big are the Soviet and East Euroepan Economies?*, Report No. 52, Washington, D.C., PlanEcon, December 1990.

Roland, G., "Gorbachev and the Common European Home: The Convergence Debate Revived?," *Kyklos*, 43 (Fasc. 3, 1990), pp. 385-409.

Romer, P.M., "Increasing Returns and Long-Run Growth," *Journal of Political Economy*, 94 (No. 5, 1986), pp. 1002-1037.

———, "Growth Based on Increasing Returns Due to Specialization," *The American Economic Review* (Papers and Proceedings), 77 (No. 2, 1987), pp. 56-62.

———, "Increasing Returns and New Developments in the Theory of Growth," National Bureau of Economic Research Working Paper No. 3098, Cambridge, Mass., National Bureau of Economic Research, September 1989a.

———, "Capital Accumulation in the Theory of Long-Run Growth," in R.J. Barro, ed., *Modern Business Cycle Theory*, Cambridge, Mass., Harvard University Press, 1989b.

Ruffin, R.J., "Growth and the Long-Run Theory of International Capital Movements," *The American Economic Review*, 69 (No. 5, 1979), pp. 832-842.

Spulber, N., and I. Horowitz, *Quantitative Economic Policy and Planning*, New York, Norton, 1976.

Summers R., and A. Heston, "A New Set of International Comparisons of Real Product and Prices: Estimates for 130 Countries, 1950-1985," *The Review of Income and Wealth*, Series 34 (No. 1, 1988), pp. 1-25.

Svensson, L.E.O., and A. Razin, "The Current Account and Productivity Changes: A Diagrammatic Note," Tel Aviv, Foder Institute for Economic Research, Faculty of Social Science, Tel Aviv University, Working Paper No. 21, 1982.

Tinbergen, J., "Do Communist and Free Economies Show a Converging Pattern?," *Soviet Studies*, 12 (No. 4, 1961), pp. 333-341.

Tobin, J., "A General Equilibrium Approach to Monetary Theory," *Journal of Money, Credit, and Banking*, 1 (No. 1, 1969), pp. 15-29.

United Nations Economic Commission for Europe, *Economic Survey of Europe in 1989-1990*, Geneva, United Nations, 1990.

United Nations Development Programme, *Human Development Report*, New York, 1990.

Urquhart, M.C., "New Estimates of Gross National Product, Canada, 1870-1926: Some Implications for Canadian Development," in S.L. Engerman and R.E. Gallman, eds., *Long-Term Factors in American Economic Growth*, Chicago, The University of Chicago Press, 1986.

Wharton Econometric Forecasting Associates (WEFA), *World Economic Outlook*, Bala Cynwyd, Penna., Wharton Econometric Forecasting Associates, October 1990.

Wolff, E.N., "Capital Formation and Long-Term Productivity Growth: A Comparison of Seven Countries," Economic Research Report No. 87-37, New York, New York University, September 1987.

World Bank, *World Development Report 1989*, New York, Oxford University Press for the World Bank, 1990.

Wyplosz, C., "Post-Reform East and West: Capital Accumulation and the Labor Mobility Constraint," paper presented at the Conference on Building the New Europe, Rome, January 7-9, 1991.

PUBLICATIONS OF THE INTERNATIONAL FINANCE SECTION

Notice to Contributors

The International Finance Section publishes papers in four series: ESSAYS IN INTERNATIONAL FINANCE, PRINCETON STUDIES IN INTERNATIONAL FINANCE, and SPECIAL PAPERS IN INTERNATIONAL ECONOMICS contain new work not published elsewhere. REPRINTS IN INTERNATIONAL FINANCE reproduce journal articles previously published by Princeton faculty members associated with the Section. The Section welcomes the submission of manuscripts for publication under the following guidelines:

ESSAYS are meant to disseminate new views about international financial matters and should be accessible to well-informed nonspecialists as well as to professional economists. Technical terms, tables, and charts should be used sparingly; mathematics should be avoided.

STUDIES are devoted to new research on international finance, with preference given to empirical work. They should be comparable in originality and technical proficiency to papers published in leading economic journals. They should be of medium length, longer than a journal article but shorter than a book.

SPECIAL PAPERS are surveys of research on particular topics and should be suitable for use in undergraduate courses. They may be concerned with international trade as well as international finance. They should also be of medium length.

Manuscripts should be submitted in triplicate, typed single sided and double spaced throughout on 8½ by 11 white bond paper. Publication can be expedited if manuscripts are computer keyboarded in WordPerfect 5.1 or a compatible program. Additional instructions and a style guide are available from the Section.

How to Obtain Publications

The Section's publications are distributed free of charge to college, university, and public libraries and to nongovernmental, nonprofit research institutions. Eligible institutions may ask to be placed on the Section's permanent mailing list.

Individuals and institutions not qualifying for free distribution may receive all publications for the calendar year for a subscription fee of $35.00. Late subscribers will receive all back issues for the year during which they subscribe. Subscribers should notify the Section promptly of any change in address, giving the old address as well as the new.

Publications may be ordered individually, with payment made in advance. ESSAYS and REPRINTS cost $6.50 each; STUDIES and SPECIAL PAPERS cost $9.00. An additional $1.25 should be sent for postage and handling within the United States, Canada, and Mexico; $1.50 should be added for surface delivery outside the region.

All payments must be made in U.S. dollars. Subscription fees and charges for single issues will be waived for organizations and individuals in countries where foreign-exchange regulations prohibit dollar payments.

Please address all correspondence, submissions, and orders to:

International Finance Section
Department of Economics, Fisher Hall
Princeton University
Princeton, New Jersey 08544-1021

List of Recent Publications

A complete list of publications may be obtained from the International Finance Section.

ESSAYS IN INTERNATIONAL FINANCE

155. Stephen Marris, *Managing the World Economy: Will We Ever Learn?* (October 1984)
156. Sebastian Edwards, *The Order of Liberalization of the External Sector in Developing Countries*. (December 1984)
157. Wilfred J. Ethier and Richard C. Marston, eds., with Kindleberger, Guttentag and Herring, Wallich, Henderson, and Hinshaw, *International Financial Markets and Capital Movements: A Symposium in Honor of Arthur I. Bloomfield*. (September 1985)
158. Charles E. Dumas, *The Effects of Government Deficits: A Comparative Analysis of Crowding Out*. (October 1985)
159. Jeffrey A. Frankel, *Six Possible Meanings of "Overvaluation": The 1981-85 Dollar*. (December 1985)
160. Stanley W. Black, *Learning from Adversity: Policy Responses to Two Oil Shocks*. (December 1985)
161. Alexis Rieffel, *The Role of the Paris Club in Managing Debt Problems*. (December 1985)
162. Stephen E. Haynes, Michael M. Hutchison, and Raymond F. Mikesell, *Japanese Financial Policies and the U.S. Trade Deficit*. (April 1986)
163. Arminio Fraga, *German Reparations and Brazilian Debt: A Comparative Study*. (July 1986)
164. Jack M. Guttentag and Richard J. Herring, *Disaster Myopia in International Banking*. (September 1986)
165. Rudiger Dornbusch, *Inflation, Exchange Rates, and Stabilization*. (October 1986)
166. John Spraos, *IMF Conditionality: Ineffectual, Inefficient, Mistargeted*. (December 1986)
167. Rainer Stefano Masera, *An Increasing Role for the ECU: A Character in Search of a Script*. (June 1987)
168. Paul Mosley, *Conditionality as Bargaining Process: Structural-Adjustment Lending, 1980-86*. (October 1987)

*Publications marked by an asterisk are out of print. They are available on demand in xerographic paperback or library-bound copies from University Microfilms International, Box 1467, Ann Arbor, Michigan 48106, USA, or 30-32 Mortimer St., London, WIN 7RA, England. Microfilm of all Essays by year is available from University Microfilms. Photocopied sheets of out-of-print titles are available from the Section at $9.00 per Essay and $11.00 per Study or Special Paper, plus $1.25 for domestic ($1.50 for overseas) postage and handling.

169. Paul Volcker, Ralph Bryant, Leonhard Gleske, Gottfried Haberler, Alexandre Lamfalussy, Shijuro Ogata, Jesús Silva-Herzog, Ross Starr, James Tobin, and Robert Triffin, *International Monetary Cooperation: Essays in Honor of Henry C. Wallich*. (December 1987)
170. Shafiqul Islam, *The Dollar and the Policy-Performance-Confidence Mix*. (July 1988)
171. James M. Boughton, *The Monetary Approach to Exchange Rates: What Now Remains?* (October 1988)
172. Jack M. Guttentag and Richard M. Herring, *Accounting for Losses On Sovereign Debt: Implications for New Lending*. (May 1989)
173. Benjamin J. Cohen, *Developing-Country Debt: A Middle Way*. (May 1989)
174. Jeffrey D. Sachs, *New Approaches to the Latin American Debt Crisis*. (July 1989)
175. C. David Finch, *The IMF: The Record and the Prospect*. (September 1989)
176. Graham Bird, *Loan-loss Provisions and Third-World Debt*. (November 1989)
177. Ronald Findlay, *The "Triangular Trade" and the Atlantic Economy of the Eighteenth Century: A Simple General-Equilibrium Model*. (March 1990)
178. Alberto Giovannini, *The Transition to European Monetary Union*. (November 1990)
179. Michael L. Mussa, *Exchange Rates in Theory and in Reality*. (December 1990)
180. Warren L. Coats, Jr., Reinhard W. Furstenberg, and Peter Isard, *The SDR System and the Issue of Resource Transfers*. (December 1990)
181. George S. Tavlas, *On the International Use of Currencies: The Case of the Deutsche Mark*. (March 1991)
182. Tommaso Padoa-Schioppa, ed., with Michael Emerson, Kumiharu Shigehara, and Richard Portes, *Europe after 1992: Three Essays*. (May 1991)
183. Michael Bruno, *High Inflation and the Nominal Anchors of an Open Economy*. (June 1991)
184. Jacques J. Polak, *The Changing Nature of IMF Conditionality*. (September 1991)
185. Ethan B. Kapstein, *Supervising International Banks: Origins and Implications of the Basle Accord*. (December 1991)
186. Alessandro Giustiniani, Francesco Papadia, and Daniela Porciani, *Growth and Catch-Up in Central and Eastern Europe: Macroeconomic Effects on Western Countries*. (April 1992)

PRINCETON STUDIES IN INTERNATIONAL FINANCE

53. Avraham Ben-Basset, *Reserve-Currency Diversification and the Substitution Account*. (March 1984)
*54. Jeffrey Sachs, *Theoretical Issues in International Borrowing*. (July 1984)
55. Marsha R. Shelburn, *Rules for Regulating Intervention under a Managed Float*. (December 1984)
56. Paul De Grauwe, Marc Janssens and Hilde Leliaert, *Real-Exchange-Rate Variability from 1920 to 1926 and 1973 to 1982*. (September 1985)
57. Stephen S. Golub, *The Current-Account Balance and the Dollar: 1977-78 and 1983-84*. (October 1986)
58. John T. Cuddington, *Capital Flight: Estimates, Issues, and Explanations*. (December 1986)

59. Vincent P. Crawford, *International Lending, Long-Term Credit Relationships, and Dynamic Contract Theory*. (March 1987)
60. Thorvaldur Gylfason, *Credit Policy and Economic Activity in Developing Countries with IMF Stabilization Programs*. (August 1987)
61. Stephen A. Schuker, *American "Reparations" to Germany, 1919-33: Implications for the Third-World Debt Crisis*. (July 1988)
62. Steven B. Kamin, *Devaluation, External Balance, and Macroeconomic Performance: A Look at the Numbers*. (August 1988)
63. Jacob A. Frenkel and Assaf Razin, *Spending, Taxes, and Deficits: International-Intertemporal Approach*. (December 1988)
64. Jeffrey A. Frankel, *Obstacles to International Macroeconomic Policy Coordination*. (December 1988)
65. Peter Hooper and Catherine L. Mann, *The Emergence and Persistence of the U.S. External Imbalance, 1980-87*. (October 1989)
66. Helmut Reisen, *Public Debt, External Competitiveness, and Fiscal Discipline in Developing Countries*. (November 1989)
67. Victor Argy, Warwick McKibbin, and Eric Siegloff, *Exchange-Rate Regimes for a Small Economy in a Multi-Country World*. (December 1989)
68. Mark Gersovitz and Christina H. Paxson, *The Economies of Africa and the Prices of Their Exports*. (October 1990)
69. Felipe Larraín and Andrés Velasco, *Can Swaps Solve the Debt Crisis? Lessons from the Chilean Experience*. (November 1990)
70. Kaushik Basu, *The International Debt Problem, Credit Rationing and Loan Pushing: Theory and Experience*. (October 1991)
71. Daniel Gros and Alfred Steinherr, *Economic Reform in the Soviet Union: Pas de Deux between Disintegration and Macroeconomic Destabilization*. (November 1991)
72. George M. von Furstenberg and Joseph P. Daniels, *Economic Summit Declarations, 1975-1989: Examining the Written Record of International Cooperation*. (February 1992)

SPECIAL PAPERS IN INTERNATIONAL ECONOMICS

15. Gene M. Grossman and J. David Richardson, *Strategic Trade Policy: A Survey of Issues and Early Analysis*. (April 1985)
16. Elhanan Helpman, *Monopolistic Competition in Trade Theory*. (June 1990)

REPRINTS IN INTERNATIONAL FINANCE

25. Jorge Braga de Macedo, *Trade and Financial Interdependence under Flexible Exchange Rates: The Pacific Area*; reprinted from *Pacific Growth and Financial Interdependence*, 1986. (June 1986)
26. Peter B. Kenen, *The Use of IMF Credit*; reprinted from *Pulling Together: The International Monetary Fund in a Multipolar World*, 1989. (December 1989)
27. Peter B. Kenen, Transitional Arrangements for Trade and Payments Among the CMEA Countries; reprinted from *International Monetary Fund Staff Papers* 38 (2), 1991. (July 1991)

The work of the International Finance Section is supported in part by the income of the Walker Foundation, established in memory of James Theodore Walker, Class of 1927. The office

gene

ISBN 0-88165-93-5

Recycled Paper